Red Thread Gold Thread

The Poet's Voice

Edited by Alan Cohen

Designed by Chelsea Blocker

ISBN 0-61-530111-8

For Evie and those committed to putting Beauty into the world.

Special thanks to the following people who made this book possible.

Everyone who has made Power of Poetry the success that it has become:
the poets, volunteers, sponsors and audience members.

Luis Rodriguez, who started this whole thing by saying that the world
needs more poetry. And for his help and support specifically for this book.

David Lee and the Honorable William Kloefkorn for showing how poetry
can become a part of everyday life. For their poems, jokes, and recruit-
ment efforts.

Michael Meade, Luis (again), Jack Kornfield, Orland Bishop and the men
of the annual Mosaic Mendocino Conference for elevating the poetic
word to its rightful place and inspiring the first steps to a world where
metaphor enriches us all.

Jane Ann Ellis, who demonstrates the true path of philanthropy.

Chelsea Blocker who elegantly designed this book and showed me the
capabilities of the younger generation.

My wife, partner and muse, Evie Adelman, a woman who is infused with
art and gives it as a gift to the world. She got me out of flannel shirts and
the woods long enough to see possibilities everywhere.

And especially to the poets who so generously contributed their time,
writing, and support to this project. They are an example for us all.

The annual Power of Poetry Festival is made possible through grants and donations from the public. To continue offering first rate poets and music to the people of our Southeastern Ohio Appalachian community at no cost, we are making Red Thread Gold Thread available for purchase. All Profits will go toward the continuation of Power of Poetry.

www.redthreadgoldthread.com
www.powerofpoetry.org

Preface

Late summer, 2001. I am exhausted after a week of total immersion into dreams, mythology, song and story. There have been conflicts, made possible by all of the hundred men in attendance agreeing to the rule of no physical violence. The redwoods have shaded me and held me in their ancient embrace. They have given me the gift of total silence when I walked out of camp to be alone with them.

Now, Luis Rodriguez, social activist, author and poet, and one of the event's teachers, stands under one of the great trees and says simply, "The world needs more poetry." This statement hits my tired, ecstatic (out of my ordinary mind) core. I suddenly understand that what we all need is poesis, the nurturance of and bringing forth the creative principle that we so often put aside in our everyday lives.

Immediately Ikkyu leaps into my mind. This fourteenth century Zen monk, trickster, turn-the-world-upsidedowner, said:

Passion's red thread is infinite,
like the earth, always under me.

And I know I must bring poetry home.

Home is in southern Ohio, a land of rolling hills, sandstone cliffs, waterfalls, forests, and wildflowers. Although it teems with natural beauty, it lacks cultural opportunities. In this area, officially considered a part of Appalachia, NASCAR and the Bible go bumper to bumper toward the finish line. Starting a poetry festival here is not going to be easy.

Now, almost ten years later, with the help of friends and poets, The Power of Poetry Festival has evolved into a weekend of music and the spoken word. Performers mingle with the locals and with those who have traveled here during hikes and pot luck lunches. For two evenings the mundane is transcended and a few in the audience hear their version of Ikkyu's words, and delve deep to find the passion and poesis that runs in each of us. They have found the golden thread that William Stafford, champion of peace, self discipline and the profundity of ideas aimed at the heart and expressed simply, talks of in his work. The thread that leads through the labyrinth of our lives, back to our shining selves buried within.

There's a thread you follow.
It goes among things that change.
But it doesn't change.
People wonder about what you are pursuing.
You have to explain about the thread.
But it is hard for others to see.
While you hold it you can't get lost.

Red Thread, Gold Thread, now winding together, now diverging in new directions, hold us to the earth, to the lives we are able to live.

Table of Contents

Poets

Essays

David Lee

Bereshith: In the Beginning

I was, I believe, four when my beloved grandmother who, within the past hour, had told me I was, "her favorite little boy in the whole world," picked me up by the hair of my head and flung me into the corner of her living room in Matador, Texas and told me I must "stay there for an hour or all afternoon," expanding to the threshold of eternity, I suspect, until I learned my lesson for once and for all and promised her and Godamitey-Himself that never again ever would the words "I'm bored" ever issue forth from my lips and that I should "tell myself a joke or a story or whatever it takes to learn what He put between my ears as the greatest gift He could ever make," and I remember taking a sub - altern deity's ransom's value of time, at least up to eight seconds, searching the corner for worms I could eat and then die to show her how sorry she would be, and then turning to the problem of a joke or story, neither of which I had a goose's idea of how to create or tell except the remembrance of how Dandy and my uncles did it and how everyone laughed except the one it was about and so I created my first original story set in the churchhouse and to make it a joke I added boogers, the funniest thing I knew, and I pulled one out over a foot long and turned around and stood up in my pew and showed it to Mrs. Hartman who hated my cockle spaniel named Honey and who I knew my grandmother didn't like because she was stiff-necked and uncircumcised of heart and said it at the breakfast table and she screamed and fainted and fell out of her pew onto the floor and her snuff mop fell out of her sleeve where I knew she hid it and went clang on the floor and the preacher said, "Oh precious baby Jesus," and grandmother went "hee hee hee snort hee" because that's how she laughed and I knew I'd said my first story out loud because when I turned around she was laughing and crying because as a protestant she knew laughter was a potential sin perhaps even as evil as dancing and told me I could come out of the corner now if I promised to never say that again and I promised and crossed my heart to make it true but I told her I wanted to make up another story so I'd come out later and I did and got to tell it at the supper table and I've kept that promise for sixty years, and that's pretty much how it happened once upon a time.

_____

Prelude to an Autumn Elegy
Adolph's Lake Hills, Texas

Then let us toast John Barleycorn
Each man a glass in hand
--Robert Burns

Over a frothy mug of dark ale
after singing along to the jukebox
Ballad of Davy Crockett
Scotty Sampson said It was
a gloaming thick as a tromp
of wet wool that day of remembrance

summerfat Herefords
trundled out of the bunched mesquite
streaming the dour hill country
like a bawling blood stain
crying for another year
almost gone

the gravity tug of southern warmth
respringing eternal in the
    feathered breast
of heaven's hurly burly undulations
great flocks of geese and cranes
ripping holes through the sky
with their cries of farewell

then like a flourish of Robbie Burns' pen
sunset ripened under Venus' beauty
a dying campfire smouldered
into the waft of fading cattle cries
sweet horse breath and creaking leather
beneath a moon of the hummingbird

So sang Scotty tonight to the oaks and rills
in a birthday backdrift
to that immaculate day sixty eight years past
 when he a boy of twelve
rode bold upon a speckled horse
bringing the father's cattle in

" … I remember taking a sub–altern deity's ransom's value of time, at least up to eight seconds, searching the corner for worms I could eat and then die to show her how sorry she would be … "

Jack Kornfield

The following thoughts were first published in Rattle Conversations edited by Alan Fox:

... there is a deep tradition of poetry as an expression of the awakened heart. The very first words that the Buddha uttered after his enlightenment was a poem where he begins, "Oh house-builder, thou art seen at last" and house-builder means "the builder of this house of sorrows, you are seen at-last, smashed is the ridgepole, broken the rafters, open to the freedom of the world, no more imprisoned by sorrow am I." So his very first words were a poem and as I began to study in the monastery, I saw that poetry was really the linguistic voice of the inner life that meant a lot to me.

Abdul Kassem Ismael, the Grand Vizier of Persia in the 10th century, couldn't bear to part with his 117,000 volume library of sacred texts and poetry when he traveled, so he had the books carried by a caravan of 400 camels trained in such a way to walk to keep the library in alphabetical order. And I like it for its humor but I also like it because it speaks about how when we become a poet and when we read great poetry, we're really part of a lineage of thousands of years of human beings trying to give voice to something that's inspired or heart-breaking and often both.

I worked together with some poets like Luis Rodriguez, who you know, and Michael Meade, who's a mythologist and poet, and we work with youth, in schools, coming out of youth gangs, juvenile hall, and so forth, and one of the forms that Michael and Luis use quite a lot, is to get young gang members to begin to listen to and write poems. When you first say to these young kids, "We're going to talk about poetry," their eyes roll and they pull their backward hats down further on their heads and they seem to disappear.

And then Luis will stand up and read a poem about shooting heroin down the viaduct in L.A., and the agonizing loss of community and dignity for the immigrants, and Luis reads like a Mayan sacrifice, it's like he opens his veins and passion and love and desperation and eloquence pours out, and the eyes of the young men start to open wider and wider as they sit in their chairs and Luis reads another poem and by the time he's read four poems and starts to pass out paper, they realize, this is a voice that's in me that wants to speak, and their own voice starts to come out.

...in June of 1945 workers reclaiming the Reich's prisons in Buchenwald found poems folded into thick squares, stuffed up into the electrical wiring, so that a person locked in a cell awaiting interrogation or death would choose to write a poem on a piece of toilet paper so that their spirit facing death would never die. And so there's a kind of responsibility in poetry, if we take it, not just a political responsibility, a responsibility to love, a responsibility to our children, a responsibility to the fading iris in the vase on my poet's desk that shows me the declining cycle of my own sixty-one years.

I told her one of my favorite poetry stories. Pablo Neruda, toward the end of his life, was invited to read in Caracas, Venezuela in the great national theatre there, and being the icon and the conscience and voice of much of the Latin culture, it was filled with people celebrating him as only can be done in a society that still loves poetry in that way. And he got up and he read, gracious as he was, for quite a long time, and then he said, "Is there anything you'd like to hear?" and someone raised their hand and said, "Would you please read Poem 19 from 20 Love Songs and a Song of Despair?", and he said, "Oh, I'm sorry, I didn't bring that with me," and then 400 people stood up and recited that poem to him. And I think, oh, what a culture that is, to have the voice of the poet in the hearts of so many people.

Here's that poem I wanted from Hafiz. "A poet is someone who can pour light into a cup, then raise it to nourish your beautiful, parched, holy mouth."

" … I'm not so much a poet as a poet groupie … And so I, I'm more of a storyteller and I use poetry… to help remind people of the possibilities in their spirits and in the world."

Alan Cohen

I have charitably been called willful and tenacious, but my stubborn streak is sometimes so entrenched that lightning has to strike twice to break through.

The first time was in 10th grade, in Wanda Bowers' advanced English class. She was the epitome of the spinster school marm, tough exterior concealing a heart of titanium. One of her piercing looks could instantly turn a 200 pound adolescent male into a quivering, stuttering Chihuahua. When she wrote a couple of lines of Ezra Pound's on the board, and asked that famous question, "What did the author mean by this?" the classroom silence was tangible:

In a Station on the Metro

The apparition of faces in the crowd,
Petals on a wet, black bough.

I understood! Somehow, I discovered that my education hadn't to date killed all the metaphor genes even though I could not have articulated this. I just knew I was struck by something deep and powerful. The poetry we 'studied' for the next few weeks was wonderful. But I was working hard to craft the image of a Jock, a Spartan Warrior. How uncool to admit that I loved poetry. I stuffed the feelings way, way down.

More than twenty years later, at a workshop in New York, the leader recited:

I wake to sleep and take my waking slow.

These words were the second bolt that cracked me. This time I was hooked. It now seemed that poetry was an acceptable mode of expression, a condensed language that nurtured the part of myself that had been rotting in the dungeon of exile for so long. A sunny beam pierced my darkness and like children thinking they can walk the ramp of a tongue of light to the sky, I climbed into the glow.

Kiss of Fire

The morning rocks release last night's heat,
no longer passion, but a residual glow,
rising to meet the sun's first kiss of fire.
This desert welcomes you into her embrace,
tantalizes with rounded buttes
and sinuous remnants of the ocean she was long ago.
Her musky aroma surrounds you,
spins trancelike memories of a primal dance
enacted as a sun circle flared on blushing walls of stone.
Embossed turquoise filigrees weave poems of love
into a Kama Sutra of the canyon,
luring you further into her depths;
and you find yourself bathed with drops of sweat,
the effort of a tender and intense lovemaking.
Not the all consuming but quick ardor
of that boy you once were,
but a surrender to her, wholly and consciously,
that allows for a deepening love,
glowing like bright embers in our hearts.

Coyote Buttes
August 2000

" Somehow, I discovered that my education hadn't to date killed all the metaphor genes even though I could not have articulated this. I just knew I was struck by something deep and powerful."

Chiquita Mullins Lee

What If — Answering the Call

It was probably *The Night Before Christmas* and all those Dr. Seuss books. I remember my mother reading to me when I was three, four, and five years old. A rhyme scheme apparently took root in my mind. I was in the fourth grade when I wrote my first poem. Mrs. Travis, my teacher said it should be published. In the sixth grade, Mrs. Tuggle gave poems to our class to memorize. I still remember *If*.

Holidays inspired hand-made Christmas, Easter or Mothers Day cards. High school was fertile ground for new inspiration – puppy love. My senior year, I bought a pink composition book and filled it with my poems. At least, that's what I called them.

Senior year was significant for another reason. Mr. Hall and Miss Blaydes, my English and Spanish teachers were poetry lovers. Together with a group of us students, we published the first literary magazine ever produced at Frederick Douglass High School. We promoted it by organizing a poetry reading. I'd never read my own poems aloud before. But a group of maybe eight of us got onstage and read about the streets of Atlanta, black pride, and unrequited love. The audience loved us. Later, Miss Blaydes gave me a blank book along with a poem she'd written about me – shy in class, bold on stage.

At Vassar College, new opportunities arose to participate in poetry readings. I was writing poems and gaining confidence about sharing them. Then I made a mistake. Second semester, freshman year, I showed my poems to a professor of mine. She smiled, "It's very nice, but it's not poetry." She suggested I read some of the great composers of classic poetry, many from the Harlem Renaissance. But I was too traumatized by her criticism to take her suggestions to heart.

Gradually, my poems gathered on the bottom shelf, quietly written and tucked away.

More than two decades later, I attended a week-long writer's conference in upstate New York. I was focused on fiction and memoir writing, but would take the occasional poetry workshop. I'd stand and read apologetically, the words of my college professor always in my ear.

In 2006, the Ohio Arts Council hired me as Ohio's project coordinator for the Poetry Out Loud National Recitation Contest. I quickly pointed out, "I'm not a poet." But oh, did I enjoy the poetry recitations by the students in the contest. The two days of recitations at the national finals were mesmerizing. The National Endowment for the Arts and Poetry Foundation sponsor POL. When I heard Dana Gioia, former NEA director say, "When you memorize a poem, it's like making a friend for life," I'd think about *If*.

What if poetry has an intention all its own? What if poetry chooses a channel and patiently waits for it to open? I often perform dramatic monologues I've written based on women from the Bible, literature, or history. People have said, repeatedly, "You're a poet." I hadn't felt like a poet, even though poems still come through me -- with and without a rhyme scheme. Usually, the language needs work, revising, and time. Today, I'd tell my professor, "It's not poetry... yet." Today, my work brings me poems and I'm inspired to read the classics, find my own poetic voice, answer the call and consider, "What if?"

Sweet Opposition

I like how words wash over me,
the jumble
confusion
ambiguity.
You like your way cut clear, precise,
edges hammered,
A snip, a slice.
I ease down any familiar
path, sleeping,
still, in comfort,
knowing.
You scream unsure, but sure I've missed
the light, the right, the life, the doing.
I can drive 730 miles into
a night without direction
and still find a warm bed,
a lamp, and a glass of wine.
You shriek
arriving safely in your steady harbor
unharmed and on time.
Familiarity binds us.
Shakes us.
Your shrill warnings lull me to play past numb.
I pull you to my tender place
Chewing down your admonitions
Like bitter wrappings
and blowing them full up and
light
like bubble gum.

"What if poetry has an intention all its own? What if poetry chooses a channel and patiently waits for it to open?"

George Bilgere

I'll never forget the day I met Morris. I showed up about ten minutes early for the first meeting of my human biology class at the University of Riverside. I was a pre-med student, and I was having a hard semester. So hard, in fact, that my advisor suggested I take only Human Biology, which was a very tough course, and "something easy," like creative writing. In that term I was enrolled in the biology course and a poetry writing workshop. I had always loved to read, but I'd never written much. Certainly not poetry. But it seemed like a welcome break from the brutal rigors of the pre-med program.

So I walked into the room. The lights were down, the shades were drawn, and it was rather gloomy in there. I sat down, looked up at the front of the room, and there was Morris. The unusual thing about Morris was that he was dead. Morris had been dead, in fact, for about five years at that point. At one time he had been a janitor at the school. He'd spent his whole career, more than forty years, cleaning the hallways and classrooms of the school. He liked it so much that when he died he donated his body to the biology department. In life he had been a janitor. In death he became a professional cadaver.

For the next hour, the instructor took me and the rest of the class on a tour of Morris. His chest cavity. His renal functions. The operations of his shoulders and arms. All you had to do was to lift or separate the places where Morris had been cut open, and there he was, inside and out. Some sort of latex preservative kept him eternally pliant. We could even look at his brain, simply by removing the top of his skull. It was one of the most amazing, disturbing experiences of my life.

So the next day, when the poetry instructor asked us to write a poem about an experience that changed us in some profound way, I wrote a poem called "Opening Morris." And it was a hit. The instructor praised it, a couple of good-looking coeds in the class told me it was great. And that was it. Biology was a struggle. I was getting Bs and Cs. But suddenly I was being praised! I was kind of good at something!

Biology lasted another semester, and I was done for. I'd been bitten by the poetry bug, and I never went back to pre-med, which is a very fortunate thing for the sick people of the world. Sadly, I've lost the poem about Morris. I owe that poem—and Morris—a real debt. But that summer I worked in a convalescent hospital as a "feeder." I spoon fed old people who could no longer feed themselves. It was another amazing experience. I talked every day to people in their eighties, nineties, even a couple of women who were over a hundred. Many years later I remembered that experience in the poem included here, "Sunset Knoll."

Sunset Knoll

When the smoking hot barrista
    Pushes my toasted bagel across the counter to me
Without so much as a glance
Because all her pistils and stamens and sweet
    Pink petals are on orange alert
For the punker next to me, Armaggedon
    Tattooed on his arms, and furthermore
She's even forgotten the cream cheese,
    Because I've reached the age
When I'm, like, totally invisible to her,
I briefly consider
    Picking up the plate and smashing it
Through the countertop, sending a rain
    Of glass onto the teabiscuits and cinnamon
scones.
That'd show her, all right.
Then I remember
    My summer as a feeder
In that nursing home back in L.A.,
    Spooning whipped ham into the mouth-holes
Of those bedridden husks of papier mâché.
How sometimes the old guys would pull out
    Their dentures and throw them across the room
Just for the hell of it, just to remind me
    I'm still here, you little shit.
So,
    Thanks, I say
And walk back to my table.
    Like I needed the cream cheese anyway.

" The instructor praised it,
a couple of good-looking
coeds in the class told me it
was great. And that was it."

Peggy Shumaker

Harriet Genevieve Langley Moen

Nestled on her lap, stroking the velvety dewlap under her chin, I took in every word my grandmother read. She taught me the cadences of language, the dance of words. I memorized my favorites, and "read" them to a carefully arranged audience--Margaret, the dog whose puppies came out a zipper in her back; Homemade Lamb, whose corduroy had all the wales worn off; and Pepi, our slobbery boxer dog.

Later, she kept teaching me to read, sending me books for every birthday, every Christmas. I saw her reading every day I spent in her company. I inflicted on her my juvenilia, and she found in it whatever potential it possessed (and some she added). She showed me her own early poems, dismissing them as doggerel, and smiled shyly when I found things to praise.

When I was in graduate school, she sent me, long before any of my friends had read it, a novel by Milan Kundera. Her note: "This is exquisitely written, but the main character has an overactive penis."

At the end of her life, we would read together, keeping company in different worlds. That time, holy.

The poem "Churning" comes from stories she told of growing up on a farm near Rocklake, North Dakota, in the teens and twenties of the last century. Ruth, Harriet, Barbara, Mary, Winifred, Joyce, Jean--the beautiful and much-gossiped-about Langley sisters.

She continues, as my imagined ideal reader, to teach me.

Churning

Long before she stood at the counter
of the cream station in a rubber apron,
skimmed up a sample for the centrifuge,
whirled it, and slipped in two drops of ruby oil,
set the points of the calipers
just so, careful as a snake
balancing an egg on its fangs,
delicate, the farmer watching
not that he didn't trust E. J.'s daughter
you understand but business
is business and butterfat
determines how many sacks
of flour and meal
go home in that wagon &
whether or not
a few yards will unwind
from the bolt of muslin, new
cloth for Easter, fresh skirt
for his wife's made-over
go-to-meeting dress
and the good part of the old skirt
whipped up into a waistcoat
for the baby, before that,
before prices she quoted
let Harriet know
whose skinny cow
wouldn't make it through
another Dakota winter, and whose
skinny kids wouldn't have a baked potato
to bring to school, before all that
she had one big chore--
butter.

After her father milked, & set
tall cans in the pantry,
it was her job
to scoop off
risen cream with a slotted spoon,
slip it into a half gallon
mason jar, and shake.
Forever. Shake steady,
shake long, shake

till her arms
fell off.
First she'd slosh
white water,
rapids foaming,
then watch storm clouds
thundering, then witness
the miraculous conception—
gold, arising
via her muscles, her
shaking, her will—
flecks to clumps to a solid chunk
new body luscious,
prepared to anoint
hot bread, huge farm bowls
of mashed potatoes,
legions of string beans.
Whatever the seven sisters,
their parents, and the hired hands
couldn't eat, she got to sell.
What did she save her pennies for?
Crank and a paddle—
                    a mail-order churn.

" ... I took in every word my
grandmother read. She taught
me the cadences of language,
the dance of words."

Assef Al-Jundi

While growing up in Syria, writing poetry was as far away from my mind as San Antonio, Texas! In those days, I channeled my creative energy through painting with water colors, and drawing caricatures.

I started writing poetry in the U.S. at a point in my life when I was struggling to determine "the color of my parachute". Electrical Engineering and corporate America were career choices that no longer satisfied me. I was looking for an appealing intersection, so I could get off the road I was on and start a new journey.

When the revelation came, it was astonishingly satisfying, and deeply emotional. At that time, more than twenty five years ago, I had written a few love "poems" to Sara, who would later become my wife and best friend. I had also written a few poems in Arabic (Even though Arabic literature was not my strong suit in the days of high school). I sent some of those to my father, Ali Al-Jundi, an accomplished Syrian Poet, for his opinion. With good natured humor, he politely advised me to stick to my day job.

My intuitive attraction to poetry which was gaining energy, suddenly attained clarity and form when I realized that my spirit wanted to sing its verses in English!

I credit my dear friend and mentor, the vastly accomplished Naomi Shihab-Nye, with recognizing a potential in my vivacious but unpolished early works, and with nurturing my confidence in my abilities.

If I have to state why I love poetry, and why I chose it to be the medium for my creative energy, I would start by saying: Poetry chose me!

As for a more rational explanation, I would say poetry is the perfect match for the idealist in me. The one who wants to contribute to making the world a better place. Our planet as a whole, and The Middle East in particular, so desperately need to move toward peace.

But even when "reality" mocks the idealist almost to the point of retreat, I remind myself that small pleasures do count. I liken myself to a farmer with a fruit stand of ripe peaches and juicy apricots on the side of the road. Tasting those nectars of sweet alphabets is sure to make someone's day!

Silly Romantic

How light can I get?
How silly romantic?
How much love
can I feel?

I am
a happy fool
and I don't care

I feel her amorous fingers
on my face with kisses
of morning sun

I see her
dancing
in swaying
gauzy
threads

I hear her
with every whisper
of breeze
through
playful
chimes

I am cradled in this moment

I do not know

I do not need
or want to know
anything
but
love

" I liken myself to a farmer with a fruit stand of ripe peaches and juicy apricots on the side of the road. Tasting those nectars of sweet alphabets is sure to make someone's day!"

William Kloefkorn

As a youngster back home in Kansas I haunted the drugstore and the pool hall and the barber shop, the filling stations and the depot and the grocery stores, listening to the metrical hijinks of the pinball machine and the pool table and the scissors and the strop and the gas pump and the telegraph and the cash register, not to mention the voices of mostly men who wielded the implements and who seemed to have an answer, or at least a refutation, or maybe a justification, for pretty much everything. So-and-so at the domino table in the pool hall, for example, is losing because he don't know his ass from his elbow, while in the drugstore the pharmacist tells a client that, yes, he'll sell him some condoms, but with this caution: using one will be like going wading with your socks on.

On Sundays the poetry was that of Ecclesiastes and Psalms, the prose that of Leviticus and Deuteronomy and Revelation. Beauty and the beast. Lilting affirmations and bewildering damnations, and ambiguities laid on as if with an immense and incomprehensible trowel. From the lilies of the valley to the bridle-high blood of Armageddon. Language, on the page and from the pulpit and the choirloft, congruities and incongruities of content and form, metaphor gaudy and thick as thieves: "For I have opened up toward heaven all the windows of my soul, and I'm living on the hallelujah side."

Much later, then, the language of Chaucer, of Faulkner and Emily Dickinson, Frost and Robinson and Hemingway and O'Connor, Masters and Mark Twain—voices with edges and attitudes I could identify with and admire and (may someone's Almighty have mercy on us all), envy. I wanted to discover who I am or might be, and what I perhaps truly believe, by way of words on the page, my own often threadbare, hayseed words. I wanted these

discoveries when I began to write, and I want them today. And because I believe that in the beginning was the music, I'd like each poem to sing, its touchstone the distinctive snick of the cueball as it cuts the 8-ball into a side pocket, or the rasp of the strop as it hones Urie the barber's razor, or...

Each poem becomes a small declaration that helps to sustain me. It becomes a shape that I can recognize and respect because it is, after all, a reflection of the glory and the jest and the riddle of its told, and untold, creators.

At The Pantry
--for Jay Gerber

Because I am sitting
in the midst of wordsong and baconsmell
  how can my cup not runneth over?
To keep it brimful the woman
whose face is mostly widesmile
tips a vessel, its contents hot and black
 and everflowing.

I order what my colleague orders,
 biscuits and gravy enough
to please if not overawe
the village mortician.

Through a window I can see that
in a farflung world
treelimbs are bending. Each time I inhale
I inhale deeply.

Thanks to Brother Parkinson
my colleague's right hand cannot stop
waving. Hello, whoever you are. Hello,
whoever.

His voice is soft and steady
and reassuring. No, life is not
yet a treadmill to oblivion. It is instead
biscuits and gravy and wordsong

and baconsmell, goodness and mercy
between us in the guise
of time neverending counting down.

" I wanted to discover who I am or might be, and what I perhaps truly believe, by way of words on the page, my own often threadbare, hayseed words. I wanted these discoveries when I began to write, and I want them today."

Don Welch

Among The Things I've Learned About Poetry

When I was young, there was something in me looking for poetry. It just didn't know where to look.

The P gene is not so rare as high school boys who think they hate poetry would have you believe.

The best poems are better than the best athletes. Take that, Achilles. You, too, Odysseus.

Good poems will outlive the longest shelves you have in your house. Short poems can have very long tongues.

What is a good poem if not a vertical moment in our horizontal lives? A few words with an articulate pulse? Words trying to deflect meanness?

People naive about words tend to swim on their own foam. They believe baubles are the soul's merchandise.

Branko Miljkovic once said, "He who doesn't know how to listen to a poem will listen to a storm."

Another poet once said that poetry makes nothing happen. Pshaw! It is a "happening."

It's happening right now in Joe and Jolene's lives.

The best readers read poems from the inside out, not the outside in. I like humble readers. More often than not they read people the same way.

I've always loved the sounds of words. Consonants which make time click. Vowels as palpable as pearls. Whole poems which are necklaces of jewels which rise and fall with my breathing. If our ears ail, don't our minds suffer?

Poems deal in quanta numbers cannot know. More often than not, if you get matter dancing in a poem you'll have a dance which matters.

Seamus Heaney says there are poems which are "pleasingly right" and those that are "compellingly wise." The stamps on the latter are the rarest in the world.

Read until you find a few poets who are writing for their lives. Dylan Thomas once said he wrote his poem "Fern Hill" 200 times to get it right. He was 19 at the time.

Everyone stands by words. Which are your companions?

_____

The Keeper of Miniature Deer

The keeper of miniature deer
was an old man with stiff knees.
He had the straight eyes of a child.
and he walked the emperor's grounds
speaking to the white swans
and the empress's pheasants.
In the compound of red deer,
among the musk and estrus,
he was especially fond of two old ones
born joined at the shoulders,
a stag with its rack huge and carbuncular
spreading out over a doe,
the old doe with eyes like fitful oil
over water. And he who knew nothing
of life after death, who lived
only to serve the miniature deer,
let them eat from his hands,
holding out salt in one,
in the other, grain,
softly calling their names,
saying, **Mother** and **Father**.

from INKLINGS: Poems Old and New
(Sandhills Press, 2001)

" What is a good poem if not
a vertical moment in our
horizontal lives?"

Cheryl Todd

Inspiration

Robert Frost wrote that "...I have worried quite a number of poems into existence. But my sneaking preference remains for the ones I carried through like the stroke of a racquet...." Poems like the ones Frost preferred seem to surge through a conduit, perhaps from an unseen power or, at the very least, from the collective unconscious. When the poems come, everything stops, and I scribble like a mad woman; if not, the words flow back into the creative provenance like the tide. Poems from the "ear of dreams" give access to things never conceived in my conscious mind and open windows to essential truths. Most famously, Coleridge experienced this backward flow when he was writing "Kublai Khan." He awoke from a visionary dream and began to write immediately, but a visitor interrupted him. Afterwards he couldn't return to the "stately pleasure dome," the "sacred river" stopped flowing, and the poem remains a mystical fragment.

After my sacred fire has been kindled, the work of revision begins. If inspiration is an alchemy that creates gold, revision is hammering the gold into a more pleasing shape. This is the time to "worry the poem" a little: to insert line breaks, to decide how to punctuate (or not), to take from and add to the poem to give it more coherence, and generally make it more presentable for readers. Even inspired poems go through revision several times. (The truth is, I never stop tinkering because I am never quite the same reader or poet when I revisit them.) At some point, however, I have to decide that they are in publishable form and send them on their way.

The revision process satisfies my logical conscious mind, but poetic inspiration touches the unconscious and fills a need to connect to a sacred source. According to Joseph Campbell, everyone is searching for this connection: "We are looking for a way of experiencing the world that will open to us the transcendent that informs it, and at the same time forms ourselves within it. That's what people want. That is what the soul asks for" (The Power of Myth). For me, poetry is not only the art I create, it is also the art that creates me: it opens the door to the transcendent. It is what my soul asks for.

_____

Sacred Fire

coming from
and going to
unknown places

slim white cloud
floating across the mind-sky
here now
gone then

soul-flower
budding blooming wilting
unseen roots
of earth

ear of dreams

reflection in a window
driving past

dandelion star
floating in a light breeze
trying to catch it complete
between my palms

" For me, poetry is not only
the art I create, it is also the
art that creates me."

Fred Marchant

Stafford and Me

I have a falling-apart copy of William Stafford's *Writing the Australian Crawl: Views on the Writer's Vocation.* Published in 1978, it was his first collection of essays and interviews. I am not sure when I first began reading it, but I have no doubt that I had studied them by the mid-1980's, a time when I first went to be in a workshop with Bill Stafford. In the layers of underlining and highlighting I did in this book, I can see the traces of the most important lessons I ever learned about the writing of poetry. I can see it particularly in two short pieces: "What It Is Like" and "A Way of Writing."

"What It Is Like" is only three paragraphs long. It begins with this proposition: *"Poetry is the kind of thing you have to see from the corner of your eye. . . It's like a very faint star. If you look straight at it you can't see it, but if you look a little to one side it is there."* What does it mean to look a little to the side of reality? Literally speaking, the "night vision" Stafford is talking about has a physiological basis. By looking a little to the side, one widens the iris and allows in more ambient light, and thus more of reality. But Stafford's proposition is more metaphorical than physiological. The work of the poem and the poet alike is train the eye to open wider, to never be content with a first glance, and never to be too sure one has seen the light. In Stafford's remark, and in his work overall, there is a great and quiet open-ness to the world and its mysteries and perplexities. One often feels, in his poems, that we are on the edge of seeing something truly miraculous. I think his poems teach us how to be ready for that moment of looking just to the side, of deliberately stretching ourselves to see what the miracle consists of.

The nature of such poetic stretching is explained in another essay in the same book: "A Way of Writing." Three or four pages long, this piece begins with the proposition that *"A writer is not so much someone who has something to say as he is someone who has found a process that will bring about new things he would not have thought of if he had not started to say them."* I have often marveled at the complex simplicity of that sentence. Complex because of its somersaulting clause structure, yet simple because it charts a most fundamental truth about writing. The very act of writing will itself generate new ideas, new feelings, new perceptions, new words. The movement of the pen across the page is perhaps slower than the synaptic firings, but the sheer physical act of writing does, I think, allow for unconscious dimensions of mind to surface and suggest new elements. For Stafford, writing itself was not a report of what he already knew, but rather was a record of his discoveries. Stafford's faith in this aspect of the writing process never wavered. It was his daily writing practice, his own way of writing. Every morning, before dawn, he would have an interval of time, a pen and some paper, and he would wait. It was like fishing, he said, and there was always a nibble. To get started, he would accept whatever came to mind, but that, he said, would help the next thing come, and the next, and thus he was off on his daily search for a star you could only see if you looked slightly to the side of where you thought it was.

When I first read these essays over and over, I had begun my own search and my own poetry, in earnest. "Bristlecone" is one of the poems I began while in a workshop guided by Bill Stafford.

Bristlecone

Sometimes a tree will be there
when you need it most, when
you realize that you've been
breathing too long in the high,

thinned out air. Maybe you've
staggered, tripped on a rock
you warned yourself about,
but tripped on anyway. Marmots

may be signaling your coming,
and you could answer with your
own set of clicks and whistles,
but all this would only deepen

the dizziness, the spin of nausea,
the dread combining with delight
at reaching the rim of the canyon.
Below, the rock shapes waver,

and you are not the first to think
they look like the dead. You want
to run after them, to tug and plead.
The feeling as it rises has its own

strong winds. You know that
lightning and rain will be coming.
You stand in one of the eroded
places seeking out that tree.

Tipping Point
The Word Works, 1994

❝ I think his poems teach us
how to be ready for that
moment of looking just
to the side, of deliberately
stretching ourselves to see
what the miracle consists of."

vie Adelman

Poetry is like milk, elemental, flowing directly from life, and nourishing it in return. It combines readily with other ingredients to create a wide array of foods. Poetry and music together sustain my being. My piano leavens poetic words with melody producing song.

My exposure to *lieder* has been episodic and sedimentary. Listening to and playing chamber music, taking classes in accompaniment at music camp as a teen, and later college classes in music literature formed my foundation. A decade later I began each day listening to Mahler songs. Still later I chanced to hear a Schubert song cycle. These songs flowed into the bed that had been carved for them. I loved the sounds of the words mingling with the notes of the piano. Now we begin each poetry festival with chamber music that opens the gates to the poetic playground where emotion and images come to dance together.

Poetry also enhances my psychology practice. I have found the way to facilitate insight for Kevin, who persists in rescuing damsels in distress, always to disastrous results. I read him Siren Song by Margaret Atwood:

"... only you, at last, alas, it is a boring song but it works every time."

And he sees.

Sylvia worries about her trembling hands as she begins the grieving process after the recent death of her husband of 51 years. I share Roethke's The Waking:

*"... This shaking keeps me steady, I should know
What falls away is always and is near."*

She no longer needs permission or a roadmap to follow her grief.

My Expressive Arts Therapy Group members eagerly write and share haiku about the past week, succinctly bringing us all into the present. The beauty of the words, the music, the art we create transcends the mundane and the vulnerability, pain and isolation of our lives.

Our Story

You swaggered into my life and
overthrew the regime

You cleaned out the closet of my dishonesties,
threw out my unbleached lies
and other long unexamined clutter

I said maybe we could have a little...
You said, Let's have a lot!

Sometimes I've wanted mush,
You offer muscle and rock.

Once you suggested, Why don't you just
play the piano for pleasure?
that mommy no longer stands in the doorway waiting
to pounce upon your wrong note

And though I tease you for your love of repetition
you became the ground bass,
deep and constant
anchoring the melody
so that it can rise and groan
and soar and tumble
and weep and somersault
and tangle and sing.

" The beauty of the words,
the music, the art we create
transcends the mundane
and the vulnerability, pain
and isolation of our lives."

Shaun Griffin

**The Working Poet: Why I Read
"New Year's Eve (1071)" by Su Tung-p'o**

When I have had a week of days and nights that will not relent, when the temptation to turn my back on this work is palpable and I am left helpless before those who would criticize, I return to "New Year's Eve (1071)" for affirmation. Almost a thousand years ago men were tested every day with the same difficult choices.

Su Tung-p'o was a public servant and the finest poet of the Sung Dynasty. As part of his official duties, he had to pass judgment on those in his charge on New Year's Eve— "pitiful convicts in chains," and unwittingly found himself their equal because unlike the ancients, he did not have the courage to free them for a spell. He was "in love with a meager stipend."

This poem embodies the two characteristics I believe to be essential for anyone who aspires to lead: humility and honesty. It is also filled with regret: without the courage to free the men for a while, he remains enslaved just as they are. We can only presume to lead with falsehoods if we forget his example.

Layered with disturbing insight, this poem reminds us that "all of us alike scheme for a meal." Perhaps the greatest measure of our humanity is how we treat those with the least among us. Su Tung-p'o helps me remember we are most fallible— whether Emperor or prisoner— when to do what is right is mistaken for personal expediency.

New Year's Eve (1071)

New Year's Eve— you'd think I could go home early
but official business keeps me.
I hold the brush and face them with tears:
Pitiful convicts in chains,
little men who tried to fill their bellies,
fell into the law's net, don't understand disgrace.
And I? In love with a meager stipend
I hold onto my job and miss the chance to retire.
Don't ask who is foolish or wise;
all of us alike scheme for a meal.
The ancients would have freed them a while at New Year's—
would I dare to do likewise? I am silent with shame.

Selected Poems of Su Tung-p'o, translated by Burton Watson, Copper Canyon Press, 1994

Running to Southern California
for my mother

Because the sycamore sky
is greased with rain and wind,
my mother steadies her house
for the return of family
from their destinations:
folk— kin— blood— beauty—
and whether we know our names
to be son or daughter
who rose from the green
and blue landscape
trimmed for the hands that bore us—
she stands, shaving onions
to enchiladas, the red sauce
dribbles to olives and avocado,
like dew in the trumpet flowers
out her window, the fallen
shoots of bottlebrush
on the tile, and when the prodigal
thrush is over,
she'll trace the orbit of us
alone on our roads,
in the comfort of dust.

“ This poem embodies
the two characteristics I
believe to be essential for
anyone who aspires to lead:
humility and honesty.”

Why I Write Poems

I developed an interest in writing poetry so many years ago that I can't remember just what it was about poems that I liked so much. I was then in grade school, and we children were probably exposed to the kinds of poems that effective teachers have always used to engage the interests of small people: rhyming jingles and the like. My mother kept a few of my earliest efforts, written for Miss Kirby, my fourth grade teacher, and one of them, now blessedly lost, began: "I love my dog / His padded paws / At Christmas he's my Santa Claus." Now, sixty-some years later, it seems that I probably came to poetry because it was fun, and in recent years I have told public school teachers all across the country that if they can show children the pleasures of poetry, they'll be lifetime poetry lovers. I think I'm right about that. Unfortunately, poetry has too often been taught as if a poem were a problem whose solution must be found, and problems do not comfortably fall into the category of pleasure, especially for small children. And once a child finds poetry onerous, the chance that he or she will turn to poetry later in life is not good.

So it was pleasure, as I recall, that brought me to reading and writing poems, and it is has been pleasure that has kept me with poetry all these years. I love and admire poems that delight me, and I entertain myself by writing some of my own. I want the poems I write to provide pleasure, for me and for my readers, and that's enough to ask of a poem, a frail thing made of words and buried in a book. I am not interested in writing poetry that illustrates theory, or that falls into the category of research, or that argues for one thing or another. My mentor, Karl Shapiro, once said that the proper reaction to any work of art is joy, and if I am very, very lucky, something I write may, for a moment, fill some reader's heart with joy.

Red Buds In January

A hundred thousand buds
on this wintering tree, and each
bright red, afire with promise.
Fresh snow, a soft silence,
and all of the greens of April
wrapped in red tissue paper
and crated in flat slats of cold.

" I want the poems I write to
provide pleasure, for me and
for my readers, and that's
enough to ask of a poem,
a frail thing made of words
and buried in a book."

Rosemerry Wahtola Trommer

Ting, ting, ting. Scott Spencer stood in the center of the ballroom, clinking a knife on his champagne glass. His father, Peter, had just married for the third time. About a tenth of the town's population had shown up for the reception—Telluride, Colorado, is not very big, after all, and Peter was known for throwing a great party. Plus, there was much to celebrate. Peter and Becky were wildly in love. It had taken them six decades to find each other, but at last, they had found their soul mates. It was as if their late-in-life love gave everyone else permission to believe in happily ever after.

Ting, ting, ting. Scott raised his crystal flute and the lilting murmur of the crowd hushed. "Here's to Viagra," he said, with an overly broad smile and a guffaw lurking beneath his words.

No one laughed. The bride's face lost its glow. The rest of us froze, our glasses still raised, unsure whether or not to bring the champagne to our lips.

Then Peter raised his glass higher and took a step nearer to Becky. Not taking his eyes off of her he said, "My luve for you is like a red, red rose that's newly sprung in June, My luve is like a melody that's sweetly played in tune …" He recited the first three stanzas of Robert Burns' famous poem, and when he was done, at least half the room had tears in our eyes. It felt like a joining of spirits again. We tipped back our glasses and drank to the love-giddy pair.

That day was the day poetry leapt off the page for me—it leapt off the page and into my ear. Poems went from things to be studied to things to be lived. I began memorizing poems immediately so that I, like Peter, might be able to pull them out of the mind's back pocket whenever necessary or desired.

While walking in spring, I might recall from Robert Frost how "Nature's first green is gold," appreciating it all the more for his warning: "Nothing gold can stay." Watching a roach scuttle to the back of an opening drawer I might announce to the air, "Don't talk to me about Cruelty and what I am capable of," drawing on Lucille Clifton's lines. One day strolling through cherry blossoms with my husband and son, A. E. Houseman came trippingly to the tongue: "Loveliest of trees, the cherry now is hung with snow upon the bough …"

The poems I have memorized, both my own and poems of others, have become lenses through which I better engage with the moment. They are frames for seeing and re-seeing the world. They offer opportunities to find the aesthetic promise in any situation, no matter how mundane or distasteful.

The pleasurable side-effect of memorizing poems is that the other author's voice becomes embedded in my own, and I find that it has greatly strengthened my own writing. The lexicons, cadences, tools, insights and rhymes of my literary heroes steep into my own lines. I have also found that when I memorize a poem, I come to appreciate its myriad layers in new ways. I never understood "13 Ways of Looking at a Blackbird" until I repeated it enough times to learn it by heart. By heart. That's what poetry's about: Feeling it more than dissecting it into its parts.

Peter's wedding day was also the day I realized how a few spoken words have the power to change the mood—of an individual or of a whole room. It could be for the worse: "Here's to Viagra," or for the better, "and I will love you still my dear till all the seas gang dry."

Peter died a few months after the wedding, and I was asked to recite the Burns poem at his memorial. I could do the first three stanzas as he did, but then knew I would never make it through the last stanza, the one he had left off for his wedding day. I knew I would cry too hard to be intelligible. So we had the poem printed and passed copies around the giant circle that had gathered at Peter's grave to say goodbye. When I came to the fourth stanza, we read the farewell in unison.

"Then fare thee well, my Bonnie lass, and fare thee well a while, and I will love you still my dear, though it were ten thousand mile."

I know Peter would have loved to have his life framed by his wedding poem. Poetry was one of his favorite lenses. (Gin, I am sure he would add, was another.)

Poetry, for me, is a practice. It's a daily beckoning to let words help shape the way we see the world. To wrestle with what it means to be alive. To grapple with what it means to die. To make this moment one we fully inhabit. And the next moment, too. And the next. It's an invitation to join our small voices in the big conversation.

The Blank Lover
Let my love be the least of things.
  —Sam Hamill

Perhaps the iridescent wing of bugs—
even the much-loathed cockroach will unfold
its fragile sheen. Or bind weed, perhaps—pink,
fluttering petals that thrive beside the road
untended, lush where nothing else will grow.
Said Burns, my luve is like a red, red rose,
but let my love be like dark soil that feeds
the fragile bloom, cool rain that soaks its roots.

Or better yet, let my love be no thing—
thin gaps between the rain drops. Not a song
itself, but breath that swells below long notes.
The faithful emptiness connecting stars
in stable constellations. Reckless wind.
Sure space between your words each time you speak.

" It's a daily beckoning to let words help shape the way we see the world. To wrestle with what it means to be alive."

Chuck Salmons

In the 1982 documentary film Poetry in Motion, Charles Bukowski (known to many as Hank) proclaims that writing a good poem is like "a good beer shit"—his point being that good poetry just happens naturally and that we know it when we produce it. While my own aesthetic appreciation of poetry has become a bit more sophisticated since I started writing, Bukowski's boorish claim, when taken in context, isn't necessarily wrong. Nonetheless, I've come to the understanding that writing good poetry is the result of hard work and dedication and can take hours, days, or even months. And sometimes a poem just doesn't want to be written. But every now and then a poem evolves just as Hank describes. And so I give much credit to Bukowski for helping revive my own interest in poetry.

When I first started writing poetry—as a college freshman—my exposure to it was very limited, primarily as reading assignments in high school and freshman college courses. The poets and poetry I knew—Shakespeare, Poe, Dickinson—while melodic and flowery, seemed archaic and difficult to dig into. Understanding poetry was like trying to get a good grip on a catfish just pulled from a lake: Even if I did get a grip, my understanding was always slippery and I faced the risk of being stung by the antennae of symbol and allusion. Understanding poetry seemed to be more work than it was worth. I nearly gave up on poetry and writing altogether. And then, as a sophomore at Otterbein College, I read a poem by Charles Bukowski in Steve Kowit's anthology, *The Maverick Poets*. I was blown away.

The poem, "The History of One Tough Mother-fucker," is a simple tale about a "wet thin beaten ... cross-eyed tailless" stray cat that the speaker takes in and nurses back to health. The speaker's new feline friend is so battered and broken the reader can only imagine that by the end of the poem it will die miserably and in so doing will offer some tragic moral about life. But in the vein of great American stories of the underdog, the cat overcomes its maladies and is rejuvenated.

In my world such a poem had never existed: the language was so direct, the narrative so relevant to my own background growing up in south Columbus, the triumph and the lessons learned so very American. That title, what guts! More importantly this poem was no catfish. It was a poem like I'd never read before—new, fresh, accessible—a poem that took risks, a poem whose speaker could have hailed from my very own neighborhood.

I read more Bukowski and other maverick poets, many of whom were part of the Beat Generation and led me to more post-modern American poetry, African-American poetry, and working class poets such as Phil Levine and Jim Daniels. Finally, I had found the voices that resonated with my own background growing up in a blue-collar family. And they have helped shape my own poems ever since.

Flame
for CM

So there's this scene in
The Man Who Shot Liberty Valance
where John Wayne steps into an alley,
and his famous silhouette pauses.
He strikes a match and emerges from shadow
seeking solace in a cigarette.
The little flame illuminates the dark hero.

There is fragility in his eyes.
As if The Duke were an aged rope
whose braids have frayed.
But in that pause,
he shows us the guts it takes
to cast aside his wooden nickel of a life
and let go the woman he loves.

As Wayne blows out the match—
like a life laid down for love—
I think of the day you left,
went back to the man who could say yes.
The fire in me did not burn

as bright, you said. If only you
could have seen what I see
in The Duke's eyes
when he strikes that match:
the longing for a chance
to let the flame inside him rage
like the fire that consumes his house,
the wedding present she will never open.

" It was a poem like I'd never read before—new, fresh, accessible—a poem that took risks, a poem whose speaker could have hailed from my very own neighborhood."

David Clewell

This Could Happen Only in My New Jersey

Shortly after the My Lai massacre in Vietnam, Bob Stephens read every word of Thoreau's *Civil Disobedience* out loud to his 8 AM Freshman English class at Highland Park High because he honestly believed that words, used well, had the power to change lives. Small wonder, then, that he was the person to show me the first poems I actually cared about in mine. I'd always been a voracious reader—cereal boxes, newspapers, flying saucer books, Ray Bradbury, even some John Steinbeck—but my brushes with what passed for poetry, grade by inexorable grade, never failed to send me running at top speed in the opposite direction: delicate flowers cracking up through the ground, winged horses in the sky. I wasn't much of a horses-and-flowers kind of guy in those days. I also got tired of charging into the Valley of Death with that celebrated six hundred every year, too (although that was hardly the good Lord Tennyson's fault). And so it was that, at age fourteen (and at 8 in the morning, remember), I first made the company of Papa Whitman, Mama Emily D. and, maybe most meaningfully, Uncle William Carlos Williams—fellow citizen of New Jersey who'd died only five years earlier. Not just his red wheelbarrow and beloved plums, either; we read *Pictures from Brueghel* and the good doctor's *Autobiography*. We even took our nutty stab at *Paterson, Book I*. And somewhere along that WCW way, I fell crazy-in-love with his pitch-perfect portrait in solitude, "Danse Russe." This poet was speaking my kind of American language, and I wanted to be "the happy genius" of my household, too.

I don't exactly know why I told my mother I was going to Mark Rosenberg's house on that particular Saturday afternoon when, instead, I hopped a bus in New Brunswick and made for Williams' Rutherford, then somehow found my way to that already legendary 9 Ridge Road address. I knew only that I wanted to see where he'd lived. After a few minutes of just standing there on the sidewalk, I was turning to head back to the bus station when the front door opened, and Flossie Williams—perhaps gleaning that I wasn't a graduate student working up a dissertation, looking for an interview—invited me inside. She talked about her husband for the next two hours, showing me his workroom, his typewriter, a few of his favorite books. I knew I should be getting home; I was taking this good woman's time. And I was supposedly a mere few blocks away at Rosenberg's. I actually said this, out loud, to Flossie Williams and, instead of being perturbed (she was fifty-something years a mother herself, after all), she offered to call Josephine Clewell and explain why I'd be running late. And although "This is Flossie Williams" meant nothing to *my* mother, that fall afternoon both she and her husband meant *everything* to me.

When I got home, my mother was less than happy. I read "Danse Russe" to her three times that night; I guess she finally had to smile. She loved me more than poetry, and she promised she'd keep on trying to understand us both.

DANSE CLEWELLIAN, OR: IS THERE A DOCTOR IN THE HOUSE
after WCW... way after

If when my wife is breaking plates and tile in the
    basement, as always
going to so many pieces for her art, her mind's
    eye already fastening on
what, exactly, might become of this legion of the
    cracked and shattered
when pressed into service unexpectedly
    together,

and our pencil-wielding son is knee-deep by
    now in his overflowing
Comic Book of Death, laughing in the face of
    the very idea, drawing
his favorite conclusions: it's either the dreaded
    high-tech plasma beam
or that 100-ton weight no one ever sees coming
    out of the cartoon sky,

and his pet mouse, Jolly—so named by his
    original, optimistic family
that finally gave up and unloaded him here,
    where he's much better known as
Not-So-Jolly—is making pint-size plans for
    another bloodletting surprise
the next time he's sprung for his daily rodent
    constitutional,

and the cat is rising above the fray before it
    actually happens,
curling up completely in the bathroom sink,
    drinking all night
from the dripping faucet, and yet surely I'm the
    one who's somehow crazy
just for thinking I really could use a cool splash
    of water right now,

and I'm afraid
the Moon isn't even half-full yet
above and beyond the summer
ruckus of cicada-laden trees –

if I, overheated in my room upstairs,
    undress entirely as a last resort,
grateful there's no mirror I have to answer to,
    waving my THE GOVERNMENT IS LY-

ING t-shirt about my head
    and singing softly to myself:
"I am surrounded, surrounded,
    I was born to be surrounded,
I am best so!"
    If I admire my Charlie the Tuna lampshade, Reddy Kilo-
watt barbeque apron,
    Bigfoot snow-globe, Dup-Nixon ashtray, Bettie Page
plenty-of-action figure,
    all of them on display in their own naked, oddball glory –

I'm no William Carlos Williams, but who shall say I am not
the happy captive of my household?

❝ She loved me more than
poetry, and she promised
she'd keep on trying to
understand us both."

Mel Bucholtz

How Walt Whitman Saved Me From the Bronx

Walking home across the Bronx one afternoon after visiting my mother dying in the hospital, a fierce rainstorm suddenly broke out, pelting the streets. Like figures from Hiroshige's People on the Bridge, people ran from doorway to doorway moving up the street. I found my way to my uncle's TV repair shop on University Avenue. Letters on the glass read: "Macphil", names of the partners, Mac and Phil.

I opened the wood framed glass door; the vacant receptionist's desk sat to the right facing the street. Gray white afternoon light stared in. The glass was spattered with rain draining down. My Uncle Phil sat on a stool twenty or so feet down the corridor out-lined by the ghostly blue light from the TV set he was working on. To his left the waist high workbench had several TV's on their sides with their cases removed, their glass tubes and frames glowing like mollusks, their electric breath humming into the darkness around them. He beckoned me in a warm friendly voice. I shuffled shyly toward him as we spoke. Then reality stopped.

I woke hearing him say the hospital couldn't send an ambulance. That he must keep my feet raised higher than my head. That I'd come out of the shock slowly, that I was alright. The rain hissed outside. My right arm ached. Walking past him my arm had brushed against the exposed chassis of a television set that was plugged in. My arm grounded the electricity, taking the charge into my body and I collapsed unconscious. I lay on the floor listening to him. As he talked to me I gazed at two stacks of paperback books next to me.

There were the 'dirty books', Battle Cry, A Stone for Danny Fisher, The Amboy Dukes, with the sexy parts soiled from being read and re-read in the bathroom. Then I found a copy of Oscar Williams' anthology of American Poetry. How could this be there?

The poetry I knew were nursery rhymes like Winkin', Blinkin' and Nod. In school we were drilled to memorize Alfred Noyes' The Highwayman. I didn't care for poetry. Poetry was memorization tests of rhymes. I opened the anthology unexpectedly to the poem There Was A Child Went Forth. Puzzled. Curious. I read about a child who went forth one day and the first thing he saw that thing he became. I was shocked. This was my life in drawing. Things I saw told me how they wanted to be drawn. They showed me how to become them to draw them. Who wrote this? Was this real? Did the writer mean what I understood him to mean?

I rushed into the other lines, descriptions of barn-yard animals, fish suspended in water, a bird singing, colors and textures of flowers; all, in their own ways, became part of this child! I was stunned breathless. This was my way of life. His words moved off the page and came alive in my mind and body. Is this poetry? No, this is truth said truthfully. True to living experi-ence. My god! Someone said it, I read it. Poetry for real!

My body felt larger, warmer and strong. My vision and hearing amplified, my mind felt crystal clear. I knew who I was for the first time; aware of feeling, knowing, and being at the same moment. Who wrote this? Walt Whitman. "I am home" rang through my body and mind, "I am home". Someone knows me. The way I feel myself in the world, first and most privately.

This is how I discovered the life saving importance of beauty, grace and wonder; of the possibilities of poetry's gift to my life, and how I became dedicated to the preservation of wonder and beauty through words.

The Body Is the Landscape of the Mind

The body is the landscape of the mind;
where the dramas of our early life
are still happening
or have become a kind of
rich preparatory engendering compost -
the vastnesses remembered
as the fruitful fields, valleys, marshes,
and deserts of wisdom
standing behind us as we are here now
present in this way
in the moment of our lives.

It is a land
where the placid and awesome features
of the yet undiscovered wilderness
are wildly flowering within themselves
for our unexpected future explorations.

And as we grow
out of our more infantile and fearful selves,
we wander into these unknown landscapes,
transformed into those sleek, feathered, scaly
and wooly animals
we really are,
the ones we are both able and needed to be
to live in those wilder, more ancient,
unknown future parts of that farther
uncharted dancing, tingling, glowing,
purple thunderous, gentle
and softly rivered terrain of ourselves.

As told by buffalo; Moab, Utah; 1985

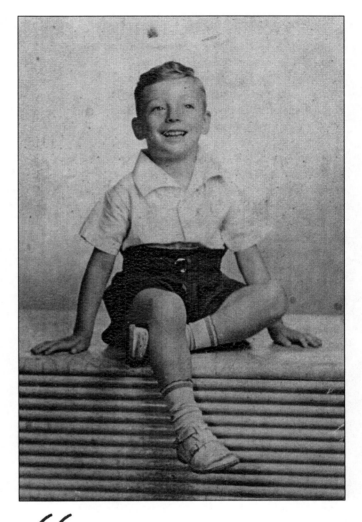

" I was stunned breathless. This
was my way of life. His words
moved off the page and came
alive in my mind and body."

Twyla Hansen

I never knew I could be a writer. I grew up in the low hills of northeast Nebraska on land my grandparents farmed as immigrants from Denmark in the late 1800s. My father had to quit school in 10th grade to farm when his father became ill. My small school district did not value literature. I do not remember nor believe we studied poetry.

It was not until I started working as a horticulturist at Nebraska Wesleyan University in the early 1980s that I received permission to be a writer. One of the perks of working at a small liberal arts college is free tuition. As an undergraduate at the University of Nebraska-Lincoln, I filled up my elective with courses in my major, horticulture, but afterward I realized how much real learning I had missed.

One of the first classes I enrolled in at NWU was poetry writing with William Kloefkorn. The year I started working there, 1982, he had just been named the Nebraska State Poet by the state legislature. I was nervous about being an older student and a non-English major, but had met Bill and was pretty sure the class would at least be interesting.

I did have an interest in poetry, too. Before I even started working at NWU, I had checked out from the public library books of contemporary poetry, including William Kloefkorn and Ted Kooser's "Cottonwood County." To my amazement, here were poets writing about dirt and cattle (or at least so I thought), and I wondered if I could, too.

To my shock, at the end of the first day of class he said next time to bring a poem we had written. I had never written a poem before in my life! And I thought he was going to teach us how! How the hell was I supposed to know how to write a poem? But that was his way of teaching writing, by simply writing. I soon learned to appreciate the beauty of such simplicity: you start writing where you start. It's that simple. And you learn as you go.

The rest, as they say, is history. I owe a debt of gratitude to all those writers who have influenced me over the years, and who sustain me still. Writing is life. Period.

**August 12 in theNebraska Sand Hills Watching
The Perseids Meteor Shower**

In the middle of rolling grasslands, away from lights,
a moonless night untethers its wild polka-dots,
the formations we can name competing for attention
in a twinkling and crowded sky-bowl.

Out from the corners, our eyes detect a
maverick meteor,
a transient streak, and lying back toward midnight
on the heft of car hood, all conversation blunted,
we are at once unnerved and somehow restored.

Out here, a furrow of spring-fed river threads
through ranches in the tens of thousands of acres.
Like cattle, we are powerless, by instinct can see
why early people trembled and deliberated the heavens.

Off in the distance those cattle make
themselves known,
a bird song moves singular across the horizon.
Not yet 2:00, and bits of comet dust, the Perseids,
startle and skim the atmosphere like skipping stones.

In the leaden dark, we are utterly alone. As I rub the
ridges
on the back of your hand, our love for all things warm
and pulsing crescendos toward dawn: this timeless awe,
your breath floating with mine upward into the stars.

" Writing is life. Period."

Jane Hirshfield

A Riddle

There are certain early Anglo Saxon riddle poems which speak from inside a reed pen, from inside the wooden plank used in those days in place of paper to carry a message. These implements appear at times more than a little bewildered by their changed fates—

The reed pen's riddle begins:

I stood once in sand,
near the sea-surge and shore,
fast-rooted in my first and innocent life.

More violent, here is the parchment riddle's opening description:

Some enemy took my life,
stripped me of world strength,
doused and drowned me in water,
then lifted me dry, set me in sun
to lose what wisps of hair still remained.
Next a knife-edge cut me hard,
scraped from me every remnant
of what I once was.

I think these passages come into my mind when I am asked to say something of how I began to be a poet because I feel that bewilderment too: poetry came and found me where I wandered in childhood's sheeps-wool pleasures, and it scraped from me the remnants of what I once was. To ask how poetry has shaped my life is no different—ask the deer tracks in snow to speak of the deer, the fox tracks of foxes. Ask a flute to explain the existence of music, or how it came to be shaped and varnished as it is.

Something travelled through me which I neither remember nor understand; I carry its story. Which somehow, inexplicably, needs us—its instruments—as well.

The Poet

She is working now, in a room
not unlike this one,
the one where I write, or you read.
Her table is covered with paper.
The light of the lamp would be
tempered by a shade, where the bulb's
single harshness might dissolve,
but it is not, she has taken it off.
Her poems? I will never know them,
though they are the ones I most need.
Even the alphabet she writes in
I cannot decipher. Her chair—
Let us imagine whether it is leather
or canvas, vinyl or wicker. Let her
have a chair, her shadeless lamp,
the table. Let one or two she loves
be in the next room. Let the door
be closed, the sleeping ones healthy.
Let her have time, and silence,
enough paper to make mistakes and go on.

" … poetry came and found me where I wandered in childhood's sheeps-wool pleasures, and it scraped from me the remnants of what I once was."

Samuel Green

When I was a kid, my father recited Robert Service poems to me and my brother in the car to keep us from fighting in the back seat. I loved those old ballads, the bounce and rhythm of them, but mostly the story. By the time I was six, I knew "The Cremation of Sam McGee" and "The Shooting of Dan McGrew" by heart, along with a dozen others. Because I could read when I was four, I also began looking for poems myself. The only other book of poetry we had in the house besides Services Collected Poems was *One Hundred and One Famous Poems* (still in print). Again, I read for story: "The Gingham Dog and the Calico Cat," "Horatius at the Bridge," "The Spider and the Fly." I memorized those, too.

I was probably seven when I discovered Yeats' "Lake Isle of Innisfree." Because I lived near a lake with an island in it; and because I often dreamed of running off to live on that island, Yeats' poem spoke to me in a way all those other poems had not. It was the first time I realized that a poem could help me understand how I felt about being alive; and it was the first time I realized I might find kindred spirits in poems. I began shyly looking for more poems that might do the same thing, reading, as Harold Bloom puts it, "to expand a solitary existence."

When I was in sixth grade, I fell in love with a pretty girl in my class who didn't return my affection. Each day I was in misery, trying to figure out how to get her to pay attention to me. Because I was one of those bouncy, disruptive kids (a year younger, because I'd skipped a grade), I spent much of the year isolated in the back of the room with my desk behind a trio of tall filing cabinets. In a way, it was a favor. I'd fallen in love with Edgar Allen Poe, and was dedicating myself to reading his complete works. One day I read a poem with her name in it, and had a sort of epiphany. Girls, I figured, were deeply romantic. Poets were romantic. If I wrote this girl a poem, I thought, she would like me. It took me most of the remaining afternoon. Here's the first stanza:

Oh maiden fair, with features kind,
thy soft black hair needs bring to thought
the touch of silken garments fine,
which in some far off, foreign land were bought.

It didn't work; that is, it didn't get me the girl, whose boyfriend tried to make me eat the poem at recess. But what it did do was help me understand that the working out of the poem answered an urgent need inside me. It met what I've since come to understand as "emotional emergency." Truth is, not much has changed for me since sixth grade. Today I still write to deal with the urgencies of joy, loss, pain, grief, love, moral wrong, the steep switchback climb or descent connected with spiritual yearning. I'm looking for wholeness, I suppose, and poetry brings me as close to that as I seem to be able to get.

Going on 27 years ago, my wife and I quit our downtown suit-jobs, sold our house, and moved onto a remote island off the northwest coast of Washington State. We lived in a surplus army tent for three years while I built a log house from scratch, using only hand tools and a chainsaw. Since then, we have given ourselves over wholly to poetry, in one way or another. We publish the poems of others through letterpress productions under the rubric of Brooding Heron Press & Bindery (Gary Snyder, Denise Levertov, John Haines, Donald Hall, Ted Kooser, Hayden Carruth, and many others); I go off-island now and then to teach in public schools, universities, community colleges—wherever anyone is willing to hire me. We write and read poetry many hours each day, seven days a week. For us, it has been a rightly made life choice.

As the first poet laureate of Washington State, I have spent the last 16 months traveling through the boundaries of the state giving readings and workshops, visiting public schools, universities, libraries book clubs and other venues. More than ever, I'm certain of the value of poetry to others. All of us who already love poetry know that a literacy of the tongue is not enough: we need a literacy of the heart, as well. I've been asked countless times for copies of poems that some shy audience member has told me speaks for them or their family.

Paul Carroll famously said that poems are tongues for the mute hearts of people.

Diagnosis
for the Opening of the New Cancer Treatment & Wellness Center,
Renton, WA

My mother said it was like having a stray
dog appear at her heels, a shadow,
unpredictable as any strange
animal in the neighborhood. Sometimes
she could hear it breathing quietly,
sometimes a restless growl in the throat.
Once it came, it never wholly went away.

It followed closest those days she gave her body up
to the care of others, room by room, secret
by secret, a world of needles, numbers and shiny
inexplicable machines. She felt, she said,
like a puzzle spilled onto someone else's floor.

I wanted to know what pulled her through.
She said that none of her doctors pretended. They knew
what walked beside her, and let her know they knew.
One by one, they helped her turn the pieces
round until she recognized herself again.

And something else, for which she had no
words. I think she wanted to say how hope
fluttered around her head like a small flock of birds
come in through an open window out of the cold.
Day after day she listened to their changing song
through all her doctors' care, the staff's regard,
her husband's patient tending:

mistake a cure remission less pain more time

My mother kept her eyes on those fragile wings stitching
together fragments of light, turning and turning
just out of reach of the dog's mouth, its sudden bite.

" It didn't work; that is,
it didn't get me the girl,
whose boyfriend tried to
make me eat the poem
at recess."

Steve Abbott

In the beginning, there was Dr. Suess. There's no question he was my gateway to poetry—rhythm, sound, and humor exploring a profound awareness of the human condition. My real appreciation of poetry came later, in high school, through a several-hundred page *Pocket Anthology of American Verse* that was required for freshman English. I was literally transformed by the discovery of Sandburg, Dickinson, cummings, Frost, Millay and most memorably Whitman. While some of my parochial school peers found the mention of breasts in "Spontaneous Me" worthy of self-conscious note, I was lifted and carried into the world of Frost's complex simplicity, Sandburg's Midwest plain-spokenness, Millay's yearning formalism, cummings' delightful wordplay, and Whitman's rhythmic cadences, the lyrical imagery that threaded through all of it fragmenting my world and reconstructing it. Metaphor began to emerge as a way of seeing the world, and with it an understanding of the interconnected web of all life. A love affair had begun.

I don't recall any particular encouragement toward poetry. I was encouraged by it. I recognized a place that I'd never been before but where I wanted to live. As I got older, I was drawn to the work of Rukeyser, Levertov, Ginsberg, Stafford, Hughes, and Piercy, realizing only later that the compassionate humanity in the work of each was a major attraction. Gradually I came to understand that the world daily offers evidence of what words can do **to** us; poetry provides evidence of what words can do **for** us.

Dog Days

August, when lawn chairs drowse
in the maple's heavy shadow
and butterflies melt in fading gardens.
Leaves hang limp in the heavy air,
and late afternoon hums a weary lullaby.
All the mowers are napping,
and even the ants have their feet up.
In the cool cave beneath the hostas,
Giacomo the cat reclines, regal and alert.
Nothing here stirs without his notice,
the kingdom unfolding as it should.

" Gradually I came to
understand that the world
daily offers evidence of what
words can do **to** us; poetry
provides evidence of what
words can do **for** us."

Laura Lee Washburn

Tongue: The Poet, That Loose-Tongued Whore

Tongue is poetry's first self, the pink muscle and sense organ straining past taste and the smooth feel of the teeth toward utterance. Tongue is a team player—no, captain of the team that makes meaning from sound. Imagine howling. Imagine saying. Imagine being understood.

The Twenty-First Century poet imagines creation at the tips of her fingers. She presses, shifts, the fingers float, and her eye begins to see what she must mean. On a good day. She remembers the woman she knew, how her husband drowned on his morning swim decades before the poet's birth. She thinks about how anger's tongue *will chew you out, berate, upbraid, ram it down your throat, rail, bless you out, take you to the carpet, scold, baste, lash, rail, give you the rough side of even its own tongue.* And she thinks about sorrow and the color of the sea:

The words she called to him were the pulse of storm, his reasons for fleeing her.
Poetry is made in the mouth.

Other days, she might find herself without words, inarticulate, incoherent. Each tap at the keyboard is an electronic blip, soon backspaced, deleted. She maunders through her lines, her lips pressed in tension. She is writing about sleep:

What the dreams mean to express is thick as school paste dried these many years in the pages of an album fat with the stored years of early life, Reminders she made for herself peek sadly into consciousness like dreams
And the thoughts give out. She's unvocal.
Tongue-tied.

Languages. Babel. The words are too hard to understand. We have yet to find the tongue in which we'll all be understood. Globally, we've agreed English is the language of air traffic control. Walking into the room, the poet sees anger in the eyes of a man. She's said the wrong words, asked the wrong question. People have made successful careers on the idea that women and men can't agree on their language, that each sex mutters in a separate native tongue.

Reading poetry in translation, the poet might find herself surprised that so many centuries or cultures away lives existed like her own. She has moments like this at home, talking to the man. She has moments like this at home, back home. And also moments when she yells or her mother cries. Critics make new language, displacing the poet, claiming prime sovereignty over *text*, that thing our poet might call, on a good day, her poem.

Tonguey: Talkative, babblative, chatty, gabby, loose-lipped, loquacious, multiloquent, talky, "You start me up; I'll never stop." The poet has so much to say. She tries and tries, hoping not to use the same words to the same effect, hoping for the little moment. And it happens again. Honestly, she speaks, says too much. The poet is a loose-tongued whore. For every insight, every beauty, all the ecstatic and religious utterances, *"Though I speak with the tongues of men and of angels,"* you'll find the harangue, whatever it is, perhaps her inarticulate love.

Fashion asks poets to claim a geography. The small salvaged Western town festers like humanity. The plains rush like grain's hush and hush across her lines. The backyard birder finds a nest in dense stanzas. The boats of her youth are moored to shallow docks, their piles of oysters shrink by the year. She has a strip mall, asphalt, steady traffic, thonged bicyclists in sea air, the desert's air-conditioned restaurant and mall. The poet's space in the world is a narrow strip of land projecting into water, the dock road, the subtle tongue.

The Mailman, 2004

"Maybe it's the gap, the feeling that someone isn't listening, doesn't get it, has half heard us, that compels us to write and explain."
—Natalie Goldberg

I was the mailman and
I thought I was carrying letters:
A, B, the whole symbolic mess
of alphabet turned to words, one
son or daughter writing from the third
world or some other pretechnological
handwritten place, but instead
I found myself
going insubstantial, literally,
believe me—it happened—
blinking out, like migraine
flashes of light that float
and disappear. Each text
I carried was blank with unmeaning.
In this century and at the end
of the last, I was noself and the words
depended only on words. I delivered
letters to boxes. Mother,
receiver of delivery,
maker of the daughter—or son—
made meaning of the blankness
of the letter, of the word: *You
know how you are, she said,
You know what you're like.*

“ Tongue is poetry's first self, the pink muscle and sense organ straining past taste and the smooth feel of the teeth toward utterance."

Tim Young

Somewhere along the wild path, a tracker will go off the trail and onto a 'run.' He follows an individual animal's spoor, rather than the wider, animal highway. Other humans might conveniently walk the trail and create a path. With repeated use, that path becomes a lane, the lane becomes a road, and, eventually, a highway and interstate. The tracker is interested in the experience of an individual being, and he knows that by focusing on the individual experience, universal experience can be understood. So, he seeks the run, follows it through tangles and obstacles, and absorbs the wild information he finds. Poets do the same.

As a teenager, I fell in love with the stories and articles in the cast-off magazines of Field and Stream, Outdoor Life, even Argosy and Saturday Evening Post. I also loved the literature of John Steinbeck, and other writers who documented the tragedies and vitality of the Great Depression Era. My grandfather told me his own stories as he rowed the old green boat while we fished together in early morning light. My curious soul sponged the characters, the experiences and the descriptions. I wanted to write about these things. But, I wanted to write the 'big' novels and saturate them with soulful experiences. I wanted it so badly that I left the university after two years, and I tried to write a novel in a cabin by a lake in Northern Minnesota. Each day I would 'warm-up' by writing a bit of poetry. I found that I totally enjoyed working on the intimacy, the personal imagery and the details in poems. I struggled with the sprawling prose I needed for the novel. After awhile, I realized that my prose was naïve, inadequately crafted and, therefore, of little interest to anyone.

When I returned to the university to learn the craft of journalists and novelists, I also worked privately on poems, as if they were my own small footprints into the wilderness of the soul. After graduating with a degree in English literature, I entered the mass communications program in graduate school, but I continued seminar work in poetry composition. My bifurcated movements brought me back to the crossroads where I would have to choose, either the chaotic, mass-media world of journalism, or the solitary wilderness of poetic explorations. One of my graduate seminars included three people who would eventually win Pulitzer Prizes for their journalism. My poetry work allowed me to personally meet many, great American poets, including Tom McGrath, Meridel LeSueur, Robert Bly, and William Stafford. By following the tracks of my own 'run,' by studying their poetry and their ways of life, I eventually found satisfaction and excitement in my own poetic life. I found friendship with other artists, poets, peers and students. I followed, like a deer run, what William Stafford called--the thread--in his poem The Way It Is. The thread has become a sturdy hand-hold for me and I thank those poets who encouraged me to follow my own thread. Here is Stafford's ten line poem:

There's a thread you follow. It goes among
things that change. But it doesn't change.
People wonder about what you are pursuing.
You have to explain about the thread.
But it is hard for others to see.
While you hold it you can't get lost.
Tragedies happen; people get hurt
or die; and you suffer and get old.
Nothing you do can stop time's unfolding.
You don't ever let go of the thread.

The Piano Player Said, It's OK

I drive muted miles from St. Paul
and listen to a trumpet on the radio.
It cries to the stars.
Even the emptiness is trembling.

Then a piano player sings,
"It's OK to be a soul survivor
on the expressway to your heart.
It's OK to lift up loneliness with a solo."

He searches each word for everyone's ache.
He opens a dark beauty
from the smallest grain of grief,
the way the ant works on the peony.

When he sings a drawn-out YOU,
an unused viol hums,
blue morning glories unfold
and the old scales soften around my heart.

" I followed, like a deer run,
what William Stafford
called—*the thread*—in his
poem *The Way It Is*."

Gregory Orr

And then that first poem. It was an autumn day and Mrs. Irving declared we'd all go for a walk—with that little suggestion. We are already breaking free of the tedium that condemned us, in those days, to seven hours a day inside the dreary architecture of the school building. Here we were, roaming the football field out back, wandering out to the very edge of the permitted. And then, past it, into the scrub woods. Not far, not more than a hundred yards. But enough for us to find a huge boulder which three or four of us clambered aboard. And then, back to the library, where Mrs. Irving sprang the assignment on us: we had to write something inspired by the walk. And so, my poem. Something fairly silly and fairly solemn. Silly in the sense that, in my telling of it, that rock was by the sea and I was alone on it and I was aware of the bleak breaking of the waves against it and the vast emptiness that stretched out before my gaze. No cliché left unexpressed.

And yet, this also: I felt enormous emotion pouring through me as I imagined that seashore scene, as I created it out of nothing but words. These weren't the descriptive words of good prose—those words whose god is accuracy and whose discipline is close observation. These were the words that created reality out of themselves. How to say that? These were magical words. These were words that had the power to create what wasn't there in reality, what was only seen clearly or glimpsed briefly in the imagining mind. And these words had the power to make what was invisible and unreal take on the substance of black marks on the page, and those marks, those words, in turn, had the power to recreate that scene in a reader. Or so goes the dream of poets. Of course, I was creating clichés. But who cares? The feelings that moved through me were very real. More real and

intense than I could ever have suspected. It was as if the imagining and the words themselves awakened the emotions deep inside me and gave them a channel to flow up and out of me and onto the page. Again, a cliché. Again, the simple truth of what it can feel like to write a poem, especially when you are young. And troubled.

As I was. Added to the isolation and alienation that are the natural state of many adolescents, I had my own burdens. I've written the poem in my journal and, as always, I turn it in at the end of the week to Mrs. Irving. And the next Monday, my journal comes back and written next to the poem in her red ink scrawl is the phrase "you continue to astonish me." And there we have a second aspect of poetry: the completed circle of expression, audience, and response. What was hidden darkly inside me brought out onto the light of the page and made into something shareable. That something, that poem, read by another person and that person understanding the words and responding to them as if they had been given a gift of some significance. And Mrs. Irving's phrase is with me still. I've let time nibble away my need for mother-love; I've let the "you" who was so greedy for attention fall off the phrase and still I find the words useful as mantra and prayer.

Now they read "Continue to astonish me." And I say that as a prayer to my muse (who is Mrs. Irving, and my mother, and other beloveds). I pray that, unconsciously, each day I sit down to write a poem. Please, I say to the muse, astonish me. Fill me with awe at the mystery of being alive, give me the words that will translate that into something I can share. Astonish me. Grant me the luck and grace to astonish others.

from Concerning the Book that is the Body of the Beloved

To be alive: not just the carcass
But the spark.
That's crudely put, but.

If we're not supposed to dance,
Why all this music?

" Please, I say to the muse,
astonish me. Fill me with awe
at the mystery of being alive,
give me the words that will
translate that into something
I can share. Astonish me.
Grant me the luck and grace to
astonish others."

Becca Lachman

One of my first vivid memories is of waking up in the arms of my father, surrounded by a congregation singing in four-part a cappella: a sleepy little tomboy, wondering—perhaps for the first time—exactly how the body creates such a golden sound and why. Raised by musicians who knew singing's power to connect and communicate, I was eventually drawn to other activities like theater and activism, roles that encouraged a similar, vulnerable listening and—most importantly—me to add my own voice to the pot. A musician's ear led me to poetry. And to be a poet is to listen to the world differently.

As a composer and lyricist, music's influence still shows itself in many aspects of my writing life and the work it creates. Choosing words and phrases for their meaning, for the way they feel on the tongue, or how they complete what I call the "pull" of a line can be a painstaking yet electrifying process. These cadences are just as important in written verse as they are within songs. Like lyrics, a poem (for me) is not "complete" until it is read aloud. Performance brings writers an audience of critics and friends, people to keep the words alive and singing, spiraling on to other ideas and conversations, perhaps into all new poems. For many years, writing and producing original musicals kept me awed by the power of words and the messages we can share. But there was more to say, so much more than could be held in a song—and so I looked to poetry.

The Romantic composer Robert Schumann supposedly developed the habit of sleeping very late into the day, which bothered his wife Clara immensely. To get him out of bed, she simply had to play an unfinished major scale on their piano, stopping just before the tonic—or final top note—was played. Being a stubbornly tonal composer, Robert could only stand this non-resolution for a matter of minutes before he would eventually have no choice but to stumble downstairs, finishing the scale by plunking out the unsung, final piano key. I love this story, and often view good poetry in much the same light: A successful group of lines brings initial discord, questioning, tension. But I look for some kind of resolution as the poem draws to a close, even if it is not the original resolution I predicted. When a minor tune ends suddenly on a major chord (as often happens with hymns), this device is called a Piccardy Third. Successful poetry can surprise us in the same way with a sudden "turn": something sweet that sneaks into a final stanza, a subtle enjambment, or a change in tone that delivers an unexpected twist about the speaker, perhaps even that connects the speaker to ourselves. As a reader of poetry, I crave this connectedness, a center on which to stand: for while poetry has a chance to challenge us and make us work to recognize its brilliance, most people come to it for a sense of clarity and human communion.

I remember first reading Sharon Olds in college and realizing that I could say anything in my stanzas! This was a tremendous discovery but also a terrifying freedom. For a young female writer who found herself in a conservatively homogenous church family that often mistrusted the greater world and unabashed individuality, speaking up in public—even on paper—meant, in some ways, breaking from my culture and community identity. An old Anabaptist proverb proclaims, "True humility is neither thinking too highly of one's self nor thinking too little of one's self, but rather not thinking of one's self at all." My work as a poet has been to resurrect this "self," to convince it of its strength *instead* of its threat. After all, what would a song be without a voice to sing it, and what would a poem be without its speaker? The beloved hymns of my youth would lose a layer of beauty if the alto line went missing. And our world— so in need of people who are willing to stop and truly listen—would lose the prophets and teachers we poets have the invitation to become. And sometimes, just to be reminded that there is music in everyday actions, that there is purpose or connection in unexpected places: this can be the poet's most important assignment.

My Mother As Minister of Music

Sometimes I think that African music
was planted like an acorn in the heart
of my white mother. Gourd-bellied Sahsahs, thumb
pianos, djembes--they'd always sat in corners
waiting. In the Mennonite farmlands of Ohio,

the need was always there
for a loud and pulsing rhythm that would drag her
from straight Protestant benches and into
church aisles 6,000 miles from head coverings,
pursed lips, and elders. Dancing joy-filled to the pulpit,
she would sing out in languages
she'd never known. Before

Africa wooed her, her
church choir belted out spirituals
but always sounded bored or desperate, singing
with as much movement as they could muster
without offending, accustomed to a cappella
harmonies, the tender blending of
human voices.

In Africa, God is deaf—the singers must
shout louder! One voice over another! And my mother
wails. My mother juts her arms into
the rafters. From that acorn in her heart,
she grows winding tiara branches, white and sharp
and sun-bleached, longing for sky.

The Kisii choir swells. She teaches them
Handel's "Hallelujah Chorus"
by rote, one part at a time. They teach her
how to sing loud and long from the very beginning
of the self, from the part that God heard
long before we ever felt
its sprouting.

“ A musician's ear led me to
poetry. And to be a poet
is to listen to the world
differently. **“**

David Whyte

We would stand barely a chance in the world if we did not rely from cradle to grave on what has been handed down from those who have lived and worked before us. From agriculture to health care, from education to sanitation, we are the recipients of generations of toil. I think of Richard Thorpe in 1667, founding Mirfield Grammar School "for fifteen poor children," a place whose doors I entered 300 years later at eleven years old, and where I was lucky enough to meet teachers both passionate and rigorous about what it meant to be a live, educated human being. I think of the library in Mirfield, a product of boring Victorian good works, but the scene of my first passionate encounter with real literature. Under a high shelf, I reached up tiptoe and pulled down my first book of adult poetry. Reading it, I felt as if I had been plucked from the ground by a passing hawk. A staid, century-old charitable contribution working its way like a wild animal into the intensity of my young life. Someone's fleeting image of a future world finding a nest in my growing imagination.

Sooner or later we admit that we cannot do it all, that whatever our contribution, the story is much larger and longer than our own, and we are all in the gift of older stories that we are only now joining. Whatever our success as a poet, we are the gift of much older work, we are all looked after by other eyes, and we are only preparing ourselves for an invitation to join something larger.

The Faces at Braga

In monastery darkness
by the light of one flashlight
the old shrine room waits in silence

While above the door
we see the terrible figure,
fierce eyes demanding, "Will you step through?"

And the old monk leads us,
bent back nudging blackness
prayer beads in the hand that beckons.

We light the butter lamps
and bow, eyes blinking in the
pungent smoke, look up without a word,

see faces in meditation,
a hundred faces carved above,
eye lines wrinkled in the hand held light.

Such love in solid wood!
Taken from the hillsides and carved in silence
they have the vibrant stillness of those who made
them.

Engulfed by the past
they have been neglected, but through
smoke and darkness they are like the flowers

we have seen growing
through the dust of eroded slopes,
then slowly opening faces turned toward the
mountain.

Carved in devotion
their eyes have softened through age

and their mouths curve through delight of the carvers
hand.

If only our own faces
would allow the invisible carver's hand
to bring the deep grain of love to the surface.

If only we knew
as the carver knew, how the flaws
in the wood led his searching chisel to the very core,
we would smile, too
and not need faces immobilized
by fear and the weight of things undone.

When we fight with our failing
we ignore the entrance to the shrine itself
and wrestle with the guardian, fierce figure on the side
of good.

And as we fight
our eyes are hooded with grief
and our mouths are dry with pain.

If only we could give ourselves
to the blows of the carvers hands,
the lines in our faces would be the trace lines of rivers

feeding the sea
where voices meet, praising the features
of the mountain and the cloud and the sky.

Our faces would fall away
until we, growing younger toward death
every day, would gather all our flaws in celebration

to merge with them perfectly,
impossibly, wedded to our essence,
full of silence from the carver's hands.

“ Reading it, I felt as if I had
been plucked from the
ground by a passing hawk.”

Garry Cooper

Poetry, Which No Teacher Can Quite Kill

In my sophomore year, Mrs. Collins, my high school English teacher, did for my love of Shakespeare's poetry what the herpes simplex virus does to genitals. Her brightly dyed red hair made her attractive to neither man nor beast, her whiplash body made her seem like a walking willow switch, and her drawn-in cheeks and pursed lips made you suspect that her only source of nutrition came from sucking on lemons. She taught Julius Caesar by having each student read 20-25 lines aloud, starting with row 1, seat 1, and proceeding in order up and down each row, interrupting only to interpolate textual comments like, "It's pronounced, 'Tre-BON-i-us' !" which was about the only laugh we had all semester.

A quarter century later, I was walking with my six year old daughter in the park near our house, and a troupe of actors, in the earliest stages of rehearsal, were reading *Much Ado about Nothing* aloud. Fascinated, Alex stopped and sat in the grass for the entire reading. She watched them rehearse and then perform all summer. Through her eyes and experience, I shook off the chains of Ms. Collins and learned to love Shakespeare. We became regular subscribers to Chicago Shakespeare Theatre, and for several years, Alex was the youngest person in the audience. She's in awe, as I am now, of Shakespeare's language, passion, humor, poetry, *words*. My job is to make sure no teacher of hers ever tries to sidle up to Shakespeare and slip a knife into his heart.

Iris Twilight

i.

Fingers raking soft across your skin,
fragrant trails smoking in the dusk.
Iris furls closely into honey-coated trumpets of the
night.
The claret fumes of Julie London kiss
the grass between the cricket's itch.
Julie nipping lightly at your throat,
night screams as Mack sweeps his emerald studded
cloak across
a glimmer at the corner of an eye.
While Iris curls, endless, just beyond our grasp,
we sweep the stars in morning's broken glass.

ii

The siren's scream,
the slender purpled throat,
Circe selling postcards by the sea
remembers in her sweep the fleets,
those constellations of our memories.
She hopes the wisp of something in her pulse
streaks softly through the ever-dying light.
So Iris draws her cape in close,
she knows the best ones never
always show the slip.
You always grasp too soon, too late
with a glimmer, tremble and a wink,
she dives forever through the echoes of Elysian
lakes.

“ My job is to make sure no
teacher of hers ever tries to
sidle up to Shakespeare and
slip a knife into his heart.”

Karen White

Writing poetry is like watching dogs play in the front yard on a late fall day. They are tumbling and growling and sprinting and you're sitting in a low lawn chair with the sun warm on your back and they want to include you, leaping across your extended legs and rolling on your feet, sticking a wet nose in your ear. Eventually they get tired or bored and amble over to the big pile of dried leaves under the oak tree and they stretch out, their eyelids already drooping, and they fall asleep. Watching them sleep is almost as good as watching them play. You hear the crows calling back from the trees and a distant mourning dove is filling in the spaces. A deep contentment settles over you like a soft shawl wrapped around your shoulders.

I came to poetry in my late 30's when I went back to college. A friend and college professor, Betty Hodges, talked me into taking her short story writing class. I had always been a reader, but never thought myself capable of the magic of writing. My stories weren't good, but the creative wordplay was addictive. Soon after the class was over, Betty introduced me to a local poet, Cathy Smith Bowers. I attended several workshops led by Cathy and discovered that poetry was what I wanted to write, and that I wanted to write for the rest of my life. Writing opened my eyes and ears and focused my attention on the present. When I walked, I noticed the mockingbird singing from the top of the telephone pole instead of worrying about how much a new roof was going to cost. I continued learning my craft while working toward my Master's degree and had the good fortune of taking many poetry and creativity classes under the tutelage of Susan Ludvigson. It was the kind and astute guidance of Betty, Cathy and Susan that gave me the courage to plumb the depths of my intuition or unconscious, or whatever you call the words that pop into your head while driving home from a late class or the crazy images that float through a wild dream. They also provided me with the tools I needed to write effectively.

During this time, I was also reading poetry and exploring the relationship of poet and reader from the reader's perspective. Finding a poem that resonates with your emotional sensibilities is better than swinging so high the chains go slack, better than hearing the Beatles for the first time, maybe even better than paddling with manatees.

The poet Ed Hirsch said, "The lyric poem is a highly concentrated and passionate form of communication between strangers—an immediate, intense, and unsettling form of literary discourse. Reading poetry is a way of connecting—through the medium of language-- more deeply with yourself even as you connect more deeply with another."

The possibility of my poetry connecting deeply with a stranger the way Roethke's poem, "The Waking," or Bishop's, "The Fish" have connected with me is heady stuff. But that's not why I write. It's the creative process. It's watching the dogs play. The poem is the dogs playing and I don't have control of them. I watch words gambol over the page and when they finally come to rest, I hear the crows.

Moonrise

Have you ever taken a wrong
turn in your mind? Ended
up somewhere you think you
recognize, but you're not
sure? Like when you go back
to your home town after twenty
years. You find "CY Strip" or some
other street that was part of the endless
loop of adolescence, where you drove,
listened to the radio and drank
rum and Coke. Instead of seeing life
like a movie, your mind keeps lagging behind
until something trips a shutter
and one snapshot appears --the vacant
brick building on the corner that used
to be Walgreen's or the white frame
house with a big front porch where you
took ballet lessons in the basement.
You're not too worried
when this happens in your hometown
because you can always find
the mountain and the mountain
is always south. But when it happens
in your mind, the mountain may not be
there, and nobody knows
where you are.
It might be foggy or snowing,
a white-out, and you can't even tell
if you're upside down. You can pull
off the road and wait out
the storm, but you can't trip
the shutter if you're standing
still. So you keep moving slowly,
from reflector to reflector, those tiny
stars that flicker on the edge when they catch
your light, until that shutter trips
and you get your snapshot, or the moon
rises from behind the clouds and shines
its one bright eye on the mountain.

" The poem is the dogs playing
and I don't have control of
them. I watch words gambol
over the page and when they
finally come to rest, I hear
the crows."

Kim Stafford

The Clock of Beauty

I was walking along the street in Oregon where two workmen were deep in a ditch repairing a pipe. It was a cold day—wet and muddy work. As I passed, I overheard one say to the other, "As the world around us grows colder, sincerity and honesty must be the fire to keep us warm."

Another time, I was sitting in a small café in Wyoming, sipping my early morning coffee. A cowboy sitting next to me turned and said, "Son, you can go down to the variety store and get yourself a little bitty alligator no bigger than a lead pencil and feed it bits of hamburger every day for a hundred years and it won't grow at all, but you start giving it whole hamburger patties on a plate and it'll turn into a goddam monster overnight—and that's just what happened to our federal government!"

After a funeral in Texas, I overheard a child ask one of the kinfolk, "Daddy, what's the most beautiful thing?" The answer given: "It is the power that comes into people at times of great need."

These speakers are my teachers—stranger, neighbor, kin. As a writer, I listen to the people around me as they offer testimony in simple, important words. I hear blessings, stories, beliefs, advice, wishes, recipes for happiness, and declarations of the good. This is my poetry. By listening to the unusual and memorable ways of saying that surround me, I learn to listen to my own quiet voice at times of confusion, consolation, and joy. I sit down each morning to write what I have heard—in the world, and in my soul.

The habit of writing poetry is how I tell time.

Lucky 4 a.m.

Little bird who wakes me in the dark,
be molecule in the bonded chain of the good.

Sip of water who refreshes,
be rain pilgrim winking through centuries.

Glimpse of gold sun out the office window
who catches breath, be one click

in the clock of beauty, benefactor of dimes
in a world of paltry millions that take us

far from what we love.

"Lucky 4 a.m." was first published in Orion Magazine.

" By listening to the unusual and memorable ways of saying that surround me, I learn to listen to my own quiet voice at times of confusion, consolation, and joy."

Laurie Kirkpatrick

Immigration

Born in 1900 in Czarist Russia, my infant father survived the diphtheria epidemic which killed all his siblings. As he told it, his mother saved him by holding onto his black, swollen tongue day and night. Dad was Milton Yawitz, a Jew born in the wrong place at the wrong time; and his childhood was so foreign to my own that his tales seemed mythological. When his father immigrated to the United States, Dad and his mother remained in the care of Uncle Zeus and Aunt Miriam. Zeus, once a rich forester who owned land in the name of a Christian, became a saloon keeper as times grew even more restrictive, and they all moved into the barroom basement. One of Dad's greatest pleasures was to go to the river bathhouse with Zeus once a week, to float downstream on his uncle's barrel chest, shower in hot water and purchase a luxurious glass of warm milk. Then Miriam was murdered in a pogrom. Dad told us that he himself was kidnapped by Cossacks, and that his mother and Uncle Zeus trailed after them on foot, pleaded with the soldiers, and won him back. However, he also claimed he could talk to foxes as a child, so who knows if everything we heard was exactly true? When Dad left Russia, he and his mother escaped through a barrage of gunfire. He remembered being carried by a farmer as they ran across a field, and the long trip over the ocean during which he stole oranges, throwing them to children in the ship's steerage.

Dad had a profound love of the English language which he embraced with patriotic zeal. He was a man who read the dictionary for pleasure, and persuaded me to study Latin in high school for its philological benefits. When, as children, my sister and I asked for scary stories, he read to us from Edgar Allen Poe while we looked up scores of vocabulary words to keep him narrating page after suspenseful page. He convinced us he'd won the heart of our beautiful and forbidden Catholic mother by writing his love poems which were kept on the shelf in the study, as revered in our family as the Songs of Solomon or Sonnets exchanged between the Barrett-Brownings. If Dad couldn't sleep, he wrote songs and playful children's stories which we found enchanting. He was a Magus to his daughters raised in humdrum St. Louis, Missouri: talented, kind-hearted and strong, but also capable of dark moods and long withdrawal. In the realm of storytelling and poetry we received his complete attention. I still keep scraps of paper on which he copied, word for word, poems he coaxed my sister and me to dictate almost as soon as we could speak. I remember quiet Sunday mornings plumped up in his bed where we wrote them together, feeling the giddy excitement and responsibility of words. It seems no accident that I came to write poetry and my sister, fiction. Read today, those childhood poems are painfully clichéd, cautious as the expression of diplomats. But whether from his genes or his mentoring, I inherited my father's love of words – the transport which carries me, still today, ever deeper into honesty, freedom, wilderness and mystery. It is he who handed me the ticket for that passage.

Quilters' Manifesto

We carried them across the Atlantic like hope:
Dresden Plate, Mariner's Compass, Log Cabin, Flying Geese.
We cushioned the Conestoga wagon seats with quilts
and wrapped our dead for burial beside the trail:
laurels for eternity, acorns for renewal,
roses for the frailty of life.
As abolitionists, we quilted for the cause;
as freed slaves, appliquéd our stories.
In Depression days we used old newspapers for batting.

Our Amish see that pumpkin and olive glow.
Our Mexicans fold turquoise and ruby mantles over Mary.
Our Hmong set the white water lily sparkling in the darkest blue.
United in a love of things shining and soft –
the quilters' flag, this coat of many colors.

Together we hold that art is to be used,
to be worn out
in the service of life:
art to sleep under, art to keep out the wind,
art to launder with the overalls and dishtowels.

Watch us squander handfuls of beauty,
like gold coins spilled into the ordinary day,
as if the patchwork fields and knotted streets
our beds, our tables, our small biographies
were precious.

Imagine what could be if we took charge,
entering the battlegrounds in legions,
arms loaded high with dazzling quilts.

We muffle the gunfire.
We obscure the borders.
We hide the enemy.

Imagine us, tireless and tender,
arresting war with beauty,
swaddling every mud-and-sweat-caked soldier
in robes of scarlet and spring green,
every life
in pinwheels and stars.

" ... I inherited my father's
love of words – the
transport which carries
me, still today, ever deeper
into honesty, freedom,
wilderness and mystery."

Mike Vause ⎯⎯⎯⎯⎯⎯⎯⎯⎯⎯⎯⎯⎯⎯⎯⎯⎯⎯

I don't know if I came to poetry because I had to memorize a couple of stanzas of Longfellow's "Song of Hiawatha" in third grade or because I was fortunate enough to have a mother who was raised with a love of poetry and passed it on to me, but I do know I've always wanted poetry in my life. As a child I wrote little poems and I continued to think of myself as a poet all through my high school creative writing classes.

Even as a Mormon missionary I recorded my missionary experiences in Missouri and Iowa in poetry. The transition from missionary to life in a university was not without a number of detours, but what finally made me give in to poetry came toward the end of my six years working in youth corrections. We had a particularly bad evening dealing with a young man from the group home at which I worked. We were handing out weekend passes to those in our charge who had "made their weeks" by attending school, keeping up with assigned chores, and various other activities required of them. If a guy fell short in any of the areas he was denied a pass. On this particular day I had to deny a pass. The kid who lost his pass decided to get even with me and came after me with a knife. I was able to quickly subdue him and he was taken to jail.

The next morning I was in my supervisor's office to fill out the incident report and found a copy of Frost's poems on his desk. My boss had gone to Kenyon College during the late 1950's and then earned advanced degrees in English and psychology. When he returned to his office and found me reading Frost instead of filling out the report, he said, "Vause you're going to get killed working here, you should go off and be a poet." I thought about what he said and decided he was right. I quit my corrections job, got a few degrees in English, and here I am.

We Were There

When I was small
My parents bought me books
My favorites came in a series entitled We Were There…
We Were There at the Alamo
We Were There with the Mayflower Pilgrims
We Were There on the Oregon Trail
We Were There with Byrd at the South Pole
We Were There in the Klondike Gold Rush
We Were There with Lewis and Clark
My favorite was We Were There at the Opening of the Atomic Era.
Little did I know living in Utah I really was There.
In elementary school we practiced air raid drills,
Every fire station had a yellow Civil Defense siren,
Buildings downtown, the library, and even some churches
Were designated as bomb shelters
People believed in limited nuclear war.
At recess, in the winter, teachers told us not to eat the fresh snow
It sparkled from radiation that floated over Utah in clouds
From A-Bomb tests in Nevada.
From where I lived I couldn't see the flash,
Feel the earth shake,
Hear the explosion,
The sky wasn't dark from the terrible mushroom cloud,
Yet across the Great Basin sand melted to glass.

“ Vause you're going
to get killed working
here, you should go
off and be a poet.”

Lynn Powell

The only books of poetry in my childhood home were a *Childcraft* volume of children's poetry and my grandfather's leather-bound *One Hundred and One Famous Poems*, which included "Abou Ben Adhem," "The Raven," and, oddly I realize now, The Gettysburg Address. Not exactly a deep and wide library for a young poet. In high school, the last poet in my English textbook was e. e. cummings, and since he, like all poets before him, was dead, I believed he had been the last poet, the end of a great tradition I had been born too late for. Still, something compelled me to write poetry passionately throughout my teenage years--without capital letters, of course, but also without any expectation that there were readers left for my post-poetry poems.

So who in this poetic vacuum gave me my first love of poetic expression? Probably my father, who had a wonderful memory for jokes and could deliver them with perfect comic timing, relishing the pun that turned listening into laughter. And my Great Uncle Duck who each month typed a "family bulletin" on sheets of onionskin layered with carbons. I remember the thrill of taking his envelope from the mailbox, knowing that inside would be a thin epistle of wisecracks, political ravings, family news, and his own cartoon censorings—@#$&%!—when the prose got too vivid for a child's or a Southern Baptist's eyes. And my Great Aunt Roxy who thought poetry "was just a bunch of foolishness," but who had the gift of telling the unvarnished truth more vividly and boldly than anyone else I knew. She could even put the preacher in his place. After church one Sunday morning, bored with his pearly gates view of heaven, she shook his hand and chided, "Well, Preacher, I sure as hell hope the Lord's got beans to break and string in heaven!" She knew that with a fresh image and a perfectly honed phrase you could get away with saying almost anything your unruly heart felt.

Tantrum, With Mistletoe

I've tried, like a peony, to explain myself
in a hundred dark petals or less.
I've been clear as the insatiable hands of the rain.
I've been Rachmaninoff and ragweed, cornflowers and castanets,
sunset swollen behind me like a red crescendo.
Yes, I've worn my heart up my sleeve. And Lord knows
I've been love's bull's-eye—
Saint Sebastiana of the Backslid Baptists.

Now snow mutes the buds and the barbed wire,
and you're out there somewhere, too, with your hot
blood and your cold shoulder, with your boots
finding fault with the garrulous white. But, honey,
what good's the last word if it just gets you gone?

I've coaxed the coals back into flame, uncorked
a sweetness even you can't argue with, and tacked up this truce
I scavenged for the doorjamb. Why don't you
come on in, and give me the slip
of your tongue? Why don't you put your mouth
where your moody heart is?

❝ She knew that with
a fresh image and a
perfectly honed phrase
you could get away with
saying almost anything
your unruly heart felt."

Michael Meade

Finding Poetry

Upon hearing someone give an example of a "found poem," I found myself reflecting upon ways in which poetry finds people. As the poet explained how a borrowed text or found object can become a new poem, I considered how a poetic line can reach into a person and reveal something hidden or sleeping in them. My experience has been more like being found by poetry at crucial points throughout my life.

On my thirteenth birthday my aunt gave me the first hard cover book I ever owned that wasn't a textbook or a prayer book. In some ways it was both of those things, but also more than either of them. She bought the book by accident, thinking it to be a history book. She was a notably short woman and in reaching to a high shelf in the store, she brought down the wrong book. From another point of view the right book fell into her hand in order to find its way to me.

As soon as I removed the wrapping paper, the error became clear. My aunt offered to return it, but I had already been taken by the images of a flying horse on the front and a mask with snakes for hair on the book's spine. The book reached out to me through her. It found me at the edge of life where childhood retreats and the turmoil of youth arrives with stirring dreams and burning questions. It quickened something in me that was waiting to awaken. I read it that night, cover to cover, compelled to enter it like a ter-

ritory just beyond everything I had been told.

The book was simply titled: Mythology by Edith Hamilton. It told tales of the Greek gods and goddesses introducing them as "strange clouded fragments of an ancient glory, late lingerers of the company divine, breathing of that far world wherefrom they come…" I became dizzy on the heady fermentation of stories, but also was struck by compelling lines of ancient poetry used to illustrate certain scenes.

On a single night, on the verge of youth, as a result of a mistake I was found by both myth and poetry and ever since I have returned to one or the other whenever I feel lost again. For me the two run together, stories and poems each trying to find us where we already are and weave us back into the stream of knowledge and into the flood of language. Each story carrying its own poesis, each poem hinting at stories under the skin of life. Each finding the other again and again in this world of being lost and found.

Mythology, a Found Poem

Despite their later rationalizing, the Greeks
did not believe that any god created the world.
For the ancients it was the other way around,
the universe creating gods after the heavens
and earth were separated. For them, everything
was shaped from Chaos brooding over unbroken
darkness until Night was born and deep Erebus,
the unfathomable underside of life and of death.

Only after the darkness became full, only
after the underworld settled down, only in
that silent, endless bosom of primal darkness
did the wind-born egg of life appear.
And, that longed-for egg, born from Night
and the underworld, burst forth as Love,
appearing first with shining wings of gold,
casting beauty in the shape of the Day,
arriving suddenly with its companion Light.

It was natural then, for the earth to appear
once Light and Love had come forth
and the darkness had receded. Even now,
if people put aside all the rationing and
rationalizing, the longed-for love and the
earth needed for its grounding can be
found more readily. The earth and love
and light are continually born from darkness
and from descent. For the human soul once
dropt from the zenith of night, like a star
falling hard from the dwelling place of the
heart of the world. And in strange ways, now
become hard to know, the gods and goddesses
are still being born amidst the wounded pulsing
of time in souls of women and men who's
task it has always been to bring these things to light.

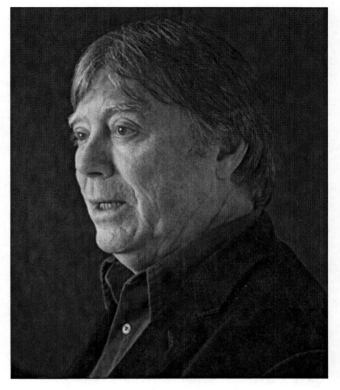

" ...she brought down the wrong
book. From another point of
view the right book fell into her
hand in order to find its way
to me."

Kim Addonizio

How I Found Poetry

When I was young and living with my parents, my father still alive and my mother also young, though I was too young then to understand how young she really was—when I was a girl and did not yet have a girl myself—when I was a young girl, my lovely living father owned a copy of the *Rubaiyat of Omar Khayyam*. The book had a brown leather cover, its title was gold-stamped, and so it was exotic. My father read to me from that book: *The Moving finger writes, and having writ, / Moves on: nor all your Piety nor Wit / Shall lure it back to cancel half a Line, / Nor all your Tears wash out a Word of it.* And in his voice that I found beautiful, my young and beautiful father said *A loaf of bread a jug of wine* and I could nearly taste the bread's sun-warmed crust and didn't yet know the taste of wine or what it meant to have a beloved. That book, those words, that afternoon when we were all so young: maybe that was the start.

Several years later I sat reading in an attic room in San Francisco and was dumbstruck by something that was called poetry—a fragment of Plath, I tell everyone, but I can't remember what poem it was and I'm not even positive it was Plath, only that some internal tectonic shift made me know I needed this thing, needed the way it changed the way I experienced life—how it made a space for my experience and enlarged it, too. That book—I think it must have been Plath—has since been lost. Soon after reading it, I would lose my father. The city I grew up in would disappear, every downtown building for several blocks razed and replaced. My mother would sell the house my brothers and I grew up in, and grow old, and I would understand something about this process but still not really understand, and I would struggle to feel the deep joy in the mystery of change and loss and not simply the terror, and poetry would help me

with this. I would discover other poets, and find my way to writing some poems of my own.

And once on a visit home I must have found that leather-bound book and brought it back to California because it sits now on my shelf with the hundreds of other volumes of poetry. On top of the bookcase are photographs of my daughter and my mother. There is a framed broadside of one of my poems, a poem about desire and a red dress, a poem written after I had tasted the wine, had found and lost the beloved.

The Sufi poet Rumi once wrote, *In truth, everyone is a shadow of the Beloved*.
And *Thou beside me*, my father read, *Singing in the wilderness*.

_____

Salmon

In this shallow creek
they flop and writhe forward as the dead
float back toward them. Oh, I know

what I should say: fierce burning in the body
as her eggs burst free, milky cloud
of sperm as he quickens them. I should stand

on the bridge with my camera,
frame the white froth of rapids where one
arcs up for an instant in its final grace.

But I have to go down among
the rocks the glacier left
and squat at the edge of the water

where a stinking pile of them lies,
where one crow balances and sinks
its beak into a gelid eye.

I have to study the small holes
gouged into their skin, their useless gills,
their gowns of black flies. I can't

make them sing. I want to,
but all they do is open
their mouths a little wider

so the water pours in
until I feel like I'm drowning.
On the bridge the tour bus waits

and someone waves, and calls down
It's time, and the current keeps lifting
dirt from the bottom to cover the eggs.

" … a poem about desire and a red dress, a poem written after I had tasted the wine, had found and lost the beloved."

David Romtvedt

When I was sixteen, I was a finalist in a program that would send two students from my home state of Arizona to Washington DC for a week as interns to our US senators. In the interview, I was asked what I hoped to do when I grew up. I said I wanted to work in "applied literature."

"Applied literature?" The interviewer asked. "What's that?"

And so I walked backwards into the world of poetry. At sixteen, I was unable to say I wanted to write. And years later, I still couldn't say it. Indeed, it wasn't until my father died when I was thirty-eight that I could tell people I was a poet. When he died, I felt relief. I was ashamed of this and to some degree still am. We are to feel grief upon the death of our parent. But I felt relief and part of that relief was in being able to admit that I was a poet, to admit that poetry meant something to me and, more importantly, that I believed it could mean something to other people. It was a pursuit worth giving one's life to. I was never able to say that to my father. He had dropped out of school after grade six and could barely read. He thought that poems and stories were useless. They didn't make any money.

As a young poet, I was afraid of looking stupid and so, in an attempt to seem smart, I wrote poems that were too convoluted for their own good. If people don't know what you're talking about, it's hard to criticize you. When I showed these poems to my father, he didn't know what to make of them and simply became enraged. The poems were opaque to him—meaningless, ridiculous. He would wave the pieces of paper in front of his face as if he could shake the poems into submission or at least shake some meaning out of them.

You can see that I think my father was partially right—not about poetry but about my poems. Little did he know—little did I know—that he was my first creative writing teacher. He woke me to the fact that poetry has to matter to another human being. All those years of my father's anger at me for wasting my life in poverty, for not going to law school or medical school or, for Christ's sake, auto mechanic school. Get a job, God damn it. Now I know that it is for my father that I write and for the men he worked with—the plumbers and carpenters and gardeners and truck drivers and electricians and janitors. When I published my first poem, he took the literary magazine it appeared in to work. He was a maintenance man for Maricopa County and I wonder what the other men thought when he opened his black metal lunchbox and dragged out a copy of an unknown literary magazine with his son's poem in it. "Weird, man. Your son wrote that?"

I did and now I'm writing for those men who had no place for poetry in their lives. These are the people who pointed me toward the injustice and the beauty of life. I want to speak for them. That I could end up a poet amazes me. I can't waste this. Not any more. I wish I had been strong enough to go in to work with my father that day he showed my poem. "Go ahead," I could have said. "Put the gun to my head. The poem can take it."

Elgin's Marble

My dad said it wasn't so much
getting old he feared as losing his marbles.
That would be the worst.

I listened to him tell the neighbor
but I thought about real marbles
and the neighbor's son who had a glass eye.
At school, he'd take it out and wave it at the girls,
chasing them around the playground. Even then
they were kind enough to pretend to be afraid.

His name was Elgin. Everybody else
was named Tony and Joe and Marcos
or Guadalupe and Linda. Elgin seemed royal.
With a name like that he should have been English
and the son of a duke or an earl
not of a long haul truck driver.

England was far from the Sonora Desert
and the bones of Father Kino in the iglesia
at Magdalena with its pilgrims on their knees
crawling toward the altar promising to do penance
if only their boons would be granted and us
on our knees, too, in the dust, marbles in our pockets
or sticky in our sweaty palms, nervous about the shot
and, if we missed, what we'd lose. Our eyes
surveyed the circle rolling from side to side.
We trembled slightly, unable to see only God
had the hand eye coordination we sought.

Still, we feigned patience, like colonialists
staring down the barrels of our rifles
at rare tigers or unpredictable wild boars.
When Elgin took his eye out of its socket,
I thought he might really wedge it between
his thumb and forefinger and shoot, but he
held back, calculating the trajectory of his shot,
promising not what would be but what would not.

" … part of that relief was in being able to admit that I was a poet, to admit that poetry meant something to me and, more importantly, that I believed it could mean something to other people."

Maxine Kumin

There was never a time in my life when I wasn't drawn to the way words worked. First, musically, when as a child I was read the poems of Robert Louis Stevenson-- I still have many of these by heart. Then, as an elementary schoolchild, the lovely singsong of Longfellow ("Tell me not in mournful numbers") and Whittier and James Russell Lowell (ah, "The Vision of Sir Launfal":"What is so rare as a day in June?" I can still do about 30 lines of this) As an adolescent, the romantic language of Byron and Shelly, enticing but puzzling. I was ripe for Coleridge's "Rhyme of the Ancient Mariner"; "Water water everywhere/ And all the boards did shrink...." Wordsworth seemed to give me permission to write, but I sensed that I was out of my depth and kept these fragments of poems in the closet. I understood that I was regarded as weird. At 17 I went away to Radcliffe, which was then the female part of Harvard, and there my true life began. Other Cliffies also loved poetry, knew poems by heart, dared to write poems. We were given to declaiming whole poems to one another. I have re-memorized about eight of A. E. Housman's poems from *A Shropshire Lad.* Since poetry is oral and aural as well as on the page, I think it is very important for it to be heard. When I was an undergraduate, we used to hurry to readings by Frost or Auden or Marianne Moore with their books in hand and when the titled was announced we would page through the appropriate text to follow reverentially along as the words were sounded.

A Calling

Over my desk Georgia O'Keefe says
I have no theories to offer and then
takes refuge in the disembodied
third person singular: *One works*
I suppose because it is the most
interesting thing one knows to do.
O Georgia! Sashaying between
first base and shortstop as it were
drawing up a list of all the things
one imagines one has to do . . .
You get the garden planted. You
take the dog to the vet. You
certainly have to do the shopping.

Syntax, like sex, is intimate.
One doesn't lightly leap from person
to person. *The painting*, you said,
is like a thread that runs
through all the reasons for all the other
things that make one's life.
O awkward invisible third person,
come out, stand up, be heard!
Poetry is like farming. It's
a calling, it needs constancy,
the deep woods drumming of the grouse,
and long life, like Georgia's, who
is talking to one, talking to me,
talking to you.

" Wordsworth seemed to give me permission to write, but I sensed that I was out of my depth and kept these fragments of poems in the closet."

James Reese _____

I'm very interested in saving voice(s) on the page, whether it's mine or say, my grandfather's or the guys' at the prisons I work with. All of us have stories to tell and to me that's much more important than a box of old photos. I like that box, don't get me wrong, but in that box, the voice is dead.

You ever have that nightmare, if you had to lose your eyesight or your hearing, which would it be? For me, if I had to choose, I'd have to say I'd keep the ears. I can't imagine a world without music—without voice.

The importance of rural voice in contemporary American poetry is important to me—here's my opinion: There is not a single art form that defines the Plains. Common sense values such as physical labor, honesty in human relations, emphasis on the primacy of family and community, and intimate physical, emotional, and spiritual connections to the land are more important now than ever. Plains art forms and aesthetics are different from urban in some respects, but we all share a special connection with the land and are concerned with preserving and sustaining our natural resources which serve as the wellspring of our most basic value systems. Poetry and prose with a Plains and rural aesthetic assert the value of the land, thus making its experience visible and comprehensible to the public at large. In this manner, poetry and prose are also capable of transcending a designation as being merely regional.

Ted Kooser has been quoted as saying, "Poetry is about communication. Anyone in the world can write a poem people can't understand." I have that quote pasted outside my office door. If Plains poetry is accessible—good—hot damn! Maybe that'll bring more readers to the big dance.

So, This is Nebraska
—For Terry, in NYC who asked me, "Nebraska? Do you guys still ride around in a horse and buggy there?"

Pa said Bobby and me could go fishing down at
Snake Creek
just as soon as we graft this here calf
and finish stacking round bales
up in the loft of the barn.

Pa said we could go play with the Indians down
the road, too,
but ma won't let us
on account of Man Sits In Tree is still fixing
to finish skinning a buffalo and make himself
a new tee pee today.

So today, like most days,
we'll likely watch them big airplanes blow by
overhead.
I wish people would just stop
every now and again for a visit.

I was fixing to go walk up the hill
and pick some cherries,
but Bobby got a tick up in his britches—
stuck to his nuttsack.
Ma said maybe he was up there
doing more than picking cherries
and won't let none of us go up the hill no more.

Ma predicts the Pony Express is due to arrive this
week.
Maybe Bobby and I can go sit at the end of the
lane
and wait for him and his horse.
It's really nifty to see him race by
and toss Bobby
our stack of mail. And sometimes even,
there's a Sears Roebuck catalog with girly pictures
for us to look at in the outhouse.

And maybe, just maybe, we could take the buggy
to town,
get us some candy—stare at all them city folk
with their fancy hats and boots.
And maybe, just maybe, we could
take on a picture show while Pa
does his business around town.
Maybe Loretta Swinson will be there in town, too.
Yessum, yessum, I do believe she's true.

> **"** Poetry and prose with a Plains and rural aesthetic assert the value of the land … **"**

Maya Spector

Some people are just word people

When I was a little girl growing up in Baltimore, my older sister not only read to me but also walked me to the library every week or so. We would hike over to Pimlico, to our branch of the Enoch Pratt Free Library, and I would get to choose my own books. That was power – having my own library card, and proudly carrying home my own books. Sometimes our grandmother would take us downtown on the bus. In those days, people got dressed up to go downtown - we wore white cotton gloves, patent leather shoes, and hats. After our lunch of chicken chow mein or shrimp salad sandwiches on toasted cheese bread in the lunch room of Hutzler's Department Store, we would go to the big library. So many books, and the science museum on the top floor! It was such an adventure.

For my twelfth birthday I received a little leather-bound diary, complete with tiny lock and key. Being enamored of Anne Frank, I named it Kitty, as she had, and began my writing life. Journaling came to be a core part of my life. I have always felt the need both to document and to process my thoughts through writing. But poetry didn't come to me until high school. It was tenth grade English with Mrs. Lee. How exactly she inspired me to write I have no recollection, but I still have the little spiral-bound notebook with my first poems. I cut a picture out of Seventeen magazine and glued it to the cover. It shows a girl, sitting on the floor, hands and chin resting on her raised knees. Her expression is, fittingly, one of angst. That is what poetry was for me in those days – a way to pour out my adolescent anguish, to express my deepest unspoken feelings. Conversations, even with close friends, did not extend much beyond who liked whom and which teachers were despicable. And, of course, how stupid our parents were. But other feelings did arise, and my private journal was the recipient of them.

What I love about poetry is its compactness, its ability to distill down the essence of something into precisely the right words. The language, the cadence; capture the spirit of the matter at hand in the most potent and economical way. It is not that poetry is more carefully written or elegant than good prose, but it embodies a piece of truth that strikes the reader or listener in a primal, essential way.

These days, I learn a lot of poems by heart, both to share at oral traditions salons and on stage in events in the San Francisco Bay Area. When you commit a poem you love to memory, it lives in your body and works on your psyche in deep ways that are hard to explain to those who have never experienced it. I highly recommend it, to those who write and to those who do not.

———————————————

Another Woman

Another woman
would keep her mouth shut,
not spout fervent beliefs
like a speaker on a soapbox.

Another woman
would have chosen
equity over experience,
settling down, or
just plain settling.

Another woman
would have stayed the course,
refusing distraction and
the pangs of the heart
that lead to upheaval.

Another woman
would not vacillate hearing
the voices that preach security and
the voices that harp on ideals.

Another woman
would not succumb to worry,
knowing that it never helps
and only constricts.

Another woman
would revel in her children's independence
instead of mourning
their day-to-day absence in her life.

Another woman
would live in gratitude every moment
for her sojourn on this gorgeous planet
and not slip into the mundane
routine of forgetting.

But I am not
another woman.
I am this woman,
led by my heart and
pulled by conflicting voices,
a woman who
worries,
mourns,
forgets.

I am this woman,
this aging, outspoken, heart-stirred,
frightened and sometimes grateful woman,
This woman,
with this particular life
and not another.

"When you commit a poem you love to memory, it lives in your body and works on your psyche in deep ways that are hard to explain to those who have never experienced it."

Primus St. John

Trail Signs I've Been Following For Years

1.Remember to follow the poem, not lead.

2.Don't forget the seasoning, the marinade and the oils in the idea.

3.Respect the language like it's fire, inattention can be costly.

4.Love the simple stories. Mighty oaks from acorns grow.

5.When cooking the poem, use your senses to marry the flavors.

6. Make it new, not customary; remember the lyric is about delight.

7. As a rule, check your equipment before skydiving. Writing is that kind of adventure.

8. Follow your curiosity; it's the tap root of your creativity.

9. Read a lot and read widely, for nutrition.

10. If you have a duty as a writer, it is to interrogate history, certainty and mystery.

11.Use solitude to get far enough away from it all, to get close to it.

12.Don't be tame about establishing and preserving your writing time. Kiss the family and say goodbye for a while.

13. When you can't write, write anyway. Failure is overrated.

14. Don't worry about your politics, others will be glad to do that for you.

15. Remember this writing stuff is just falling in love with the world's passions and trying them out in words.

_____

Today

Butte Creek has come out of the canyon
like a tongue for hundreds of years.
It is still the most beautiful voice in the valley.
Along the banks, Cottonwoods are standing
conversing with Alder and Oak.
In a few weeks their dark hair will crackle
with colors just like fire.
Right now however, they are a lush veil
below the crimped rock face
at the top of the canyon walls,
shoed in roots and rocks
and luxuriant thorny vine.
But today is the only day
in these dragonflies' lives,
and they are a thousand ecstasies
hovering above the cold clear water.

" Remember this writing stuff
is just falling in love with the
world's passions and trying
them out in words."

Coleman Barks

Breathing and Writing

I had an ecstatic Latin teacher in the 8th grade, who one fall afternoon read us Edna St. Vincent Millay's "Afternoon on a Hill." The middle stanza of its three goes,

> I will look at cliffs and clouds
>   With quiet eyes,
> Watch the wind bow down the grass,
>   And the grass rise.

Those words caught my afterschool wandering so perfectly. I felt how words and the world could sing together inside me, and I wanted more of that.

In the 10th grade Roy Ashley said we could get extra credit if we memorized Poe's "The Raven," and performed it in class. I paced drunkenly back and forth in my room saying the fool thing until it stuck there in the monkey-mind of my memorizer, those galloping triple rhymes, remember-December-ember.

Ah distinctly, I did remember, and the unbroken tidal flow of it was empowering to me, because I was a stammerer as a child, and on into high school. Stammerers never have a problem with singing. Poe's "Raven" is such a blend of spoken word with chant that it let me easily bridge that danger zone (for me) where breath moves out and becomes a public act.

So those are two times, one very quiet and one wildly flamboyant, when language (poetry) became a lively, breathable medium for me. E.E.Cummings gave me love language in college. And Whitman. Near the end of "Song of Myself" he says,

> There is that in me–I do not know what it is –But I know it is in me

That beautiful blurting out of knowing and not-knowing felt freeing to me, like a wind of honesty washing the sky.

Then there was Thomas Wolfe's prose. I rode that head of steam for a while. Gary Snyder's clear, ax handle simplicity. Thoreau. The magnificent richness of Sir Gawain and the Green Knight. Hopkins, Keats, Shakespeare, Yeats. D.H. Lawrence.

I have a lot of loves, Dickinson, Galway Kinnell. And I am still finding them. Vis-WAH-va Szymborska.

I never even heard Rumi's name until I was thirty-nine. Entering that region was like suddenly being able to breathe inside the ocean. So I gave in to it and walked around, exploring. There was a nomadic gathering of souls on their way somewhere, nowhere, everywhere. Continuously variable, I still meet up with them several times a year. My secret, mystical, intuition is that the ocean I felt that I could breathe inside was, and is, the transmitted presence of Rumi's friend, Shams Tabriz.

Higdon Cove

Give it the next fellow
Not the ten dollars, the help. No mistaking
what he meant or saw the afternoon as,
a fine chance. The 1965 tractor started up,
though one of its brakes kept sticking, amusing him.
I'd gotten as far as I could, trying to find a new walk,
to a gate bar across the road, and backed back and onto
soft shoulder, slid helplessly into the ditch, hopeless
to maneuver out of. Walked to the nearest house.
He came to the door, still chewing his lunch,
then toward the barn, I making polite apology.
You're heading for that tractor, aren't you?
If it won't start, we'll get a horse.
The man that wants no credit, or even to shake hands,
too busy with what needs doing, holds his arms
close in and sidles by me in the barn
like I'm a ticklish passage, me holding out my money.
Give it the next fellow.

There is a huge holly tree next to where I glided to a stop,
a solid thigh trunk, white-splotched
and stretching deep under the ditch water.
Beauty, but not such as this man is,
beyond any tree.

" I never even heard
Rumi's name until I was
thirty-nine. Entering that
region was like suddenly
being able to breathe
inside the ocean. So I
gave in to it and walked
around, exploring."

Alison Luterman

I fell in love with poetry very young--I was six or seven years old. Someone gave me Louis Untermeyer's anthology *A Child's Golden Treasury of Poetry* and I read it over and over. I didn't understand all of the poetry--it was a good selection of real poems, not just kiddy stuff--but I loved the sound of the words in my brain. I especially loved Alfred Noyes' "The Highwayman"--"Bess, the land-lord's daughter/the landlord's black-eyed daughter/plaiting a blood-red love knot/Into her long dark hair." I didn't know what a "love-knot" was, and the eroticism of the poem was over my head, but something deep inside me thrilled to it. So my first love in poetry were ballads. But that book had everything--lyrics, nature poems, silly poems, everything. It was a whole world unto itself. I started writing my own poetry in second grade and it quickly became an easy way to get positive attention. I remember being sent to the principal's office to show her a poem I wrote. When I was an adolescent, poetry became darker and more necessary for me--it was a place to start naming feelings and experiences I had no other language for. Decades later I'm still doing it.

Jesus Incognito

Don't tell anyone, but I love Jesus.
I love his big dark Jewish eyes, so full
of suffering and soul,
like an unemployed poet's, and his
thick sensuous Jewish lips,
and his kinky curly hair, just like mine,
uncontrollable despite conditioners,
and the way he always argues with everyone
and will go to hell for love.
He's just like that Buddhist god
Avalokiteshvara, the bodhisattva of compassion,
except his name is easier to pro-
nounce.
When you're in trouble it's hard to
remember to yell for Avalokiteshvara,
but "Oh Jesus!" arises naturally
every time a crazy driver hot-dogs past
me on the freeway.
I know I should say the Shema when
I'm about to die,
but will I be able to remember Hebrew
at a time like that?
I don't want to die saying, "Oh shit!"
I'd like to leave my body consciously,
like a Tibetan lama, sitting in full lotus
with my head turned toward where I'll
reincarnate next.
But let's be realistic: I probably
couldn't meditate enough to become enlightened
in the however-many years I have left.
Jesus seems easier. All you have to do
is love everyone.
Well, seems is the key word here.
Sometimes the more you try to love
people, the more you hate them.
Maybe it would be better to try
not to love people, and then watch the love
force its way out of you like grass
through cement.
Anything is better than organized religion.
I don't like singing in churches-all
those hymns in major keys.

I don't think religion should be so triumphant.
It should be humble and aware of the basic incurable pathos of the human condition,
and in a minor key and sung in a mysterious ancient language, like Sanskrit or Hebrew.
Is it OK for me to love Jesus but not be a Christian?
I could try to open my heart and give away all my possessions.
It's not that different from being Buddhist, after all, except for a history
of witch burnings, the Inquisition, the subjugation,
rape, and pillage of indigenous peoples all over the world,
not to mention twenty centuries of vicious anti-Semitism.
That's a lot to overlook to get back to a baby born among animals to a Jewish mother, Miryam.
And what about that other Mary, the sexy one? Jesus, I don't believe you died a virgin.
I think you needed to taste everything human, to inhabit the whole mess:
blood, shit, flies, regret, envy, why-me.
I owe you and all the other bodhisattvas and sages
and newborn babies a debt of thanks for agreeing to come back and marry yourselves
to our painful predicament again and again-
and I do thank you, bowing to the infinite directions.

" … poetry became darker and more necessary for me—it was a place to start naming feelings and experiences I had no other language for."

Thomas R. Smith

For The European Friends

Although I've always written poetry for pleasure (as a boy, I imitated the maniacal rhythms of Edgar Allan Poe), it took me until age 30 to acknowledge poetry as my path and calling. Poetry had been an integral component of my creativity throughout my twenties, along with fiction, art, and music. In fact, the problem lay partly in the diversity of my artistic efforts -jack of many arts, I'd mastered none.

I'd heard in my late twenties the view that 30 was an age for consolidating scattered energies, for identifying one's strong suit and committing to it. I carried this idea, more or less consciously, with me to Europe, where I spent a year hitchhiking around numerous countries. Midway in my travels, I celebrated my 30th birthday with fourteen young Italians in an apartment in Naples.

As a young man, I'd suffered the usual low self-esteem of the would-be artist marginalized by American society. In European society, the poet was a respected figure, a valued member of the community. My year in Europe helped me to expand my view of the poet's role and re-imagine myself as a literary world citizen.

Once on a visit to my college, Galway Kinnell, reading his newly published masterpiece, *The Book of Nightmares*, said he'd modeled his long-poem on Rilke's *Duino Elegies*. Rilke's poem represents a heroic attempt to write beyond what the poet knew personally, in other words to induce vision. That appealed to my twenty-year-old's romanticism and once rooted in my consciousness became a continual challenge to my artistic ambition.

At 30, desperate to focus and get on with the real work of my life, I chose the art that I knew had chosen me, the practice of which could take me as far into vision as I was capable of going. I wanted Blake's "bow of burning gold" to give my expressive arrows their farthest flight. Witnessing daily demonstrations of my European friends' passion for their poets and ours, I felt some great determination solidifying in me over that year. Though my European friendships did not, alas, outlive the circumstances of my travel, they left me lasting gifts of validation and encouragement for the challenging journey toward poetry.

The Reply

What good have these poems done?
The question insisted relentlessly
with every mile I drove into
strip-malled heartland that radiant
spring day. My forty-seven years,
my choice and stubborn practice . . .

Later, calmed by a motel's
plastic assurances, I slept, with
miniature golf outside the window,
and dreamt we'd been baking bread.
Our loaves stood stacked with those
of other bakers in a wall of bread,

boules like skulls, nubbled heels
of baguettes like the femurs and tibias
of those five thousand Franciscans
in their terrifying chapel in Portugal.
And I felt suddenly afraid that
this wall, our hope and common labor,

might come in the end to nothing
but bones, though when I stood
behind the wall, I saw each individual
loaf had been clearly marked with
the name of some hungry person to whom
it would be delivered without fail.

" I wanted Blake's 'bow of
burning gold' to give my
expressive arrows their
farthest flight."

86

Ellen Bass

I think poetry itself is what lured me to fall in love with it. I didn't come from a literary family, though my mother occasionally read a poem aloud, careful to read it well, as she was careful in all things, wrapping a sandwich in waxed paper or counting out change for a customer. She took a certain pride in knowing that you didn't stop at the end of a line, but followed the thought through until a natural place to pause.

We didn't have many books in our house until my brother, who is eight years older, went to college. On weekends, I'd cut myself a thick slab of salami, take a couple slices of American cheese, a knob of rye bread and a glass of milk and settle myself in the leather recliner in his empty room and read books from his shelves.

My first typewriter was a hand-me-down from my brother. I wish I still had it—a clunky black metal Remington with round silver-rimmed keys on which I taught myself to type using a fingering chart my brother made for me. Recently I was cleaning out my garage and came across a box of old papers, including some note cards on which I'd typed out poems and quotations fifty years ago:

The Moving Finger writes; and, having writ,
Moves on: nor all your Piety nor Wit
Shall lure it back to Cancel half a line,
Nor all your Tears wash out a Word of it.

Rubáiyát of Omar Khayyám

I added the accent marks in pencil and some of the letters are darker than others. The punctuation keys I must have hit especially hard because they have indented the cards with their force. I can't help but wonder what this passage meant to me then,

having had no experiences so painful that I would have wanted to erase them. Maybe I was preparing myself for the future. These lines certainly describe my struggles now—there's so much I wish I could go back and do differently. Or maybe it was something beyond the content, the way poetry speaks to us about the human condition, whether we have had similar experiences ourselves or not. All I know for sure is that I had a hunger for this kind of meaningful communication—and I still do.

If You Knew

What if you knew you'd be the last
to touch someone?
If you were taking tickets, for example,
at the theater, tearing them,
giving back the ragged stubs,
you might take care to touch that palm,
brush your fingertips
along the life line's crease.

When a man pulls his wheeled suitcase
too slowly through the airport, when
the car in front of me doesn't signal,
when the clerk at the pharmacy
won't say *Thank you*, I don't remember
they're going to die.

A friend told me she'd been with her aunt.
They'd just had lunch and the waiter,
a young gay man with plum black eyes,
joked as he served the coffee, kissed
her aunt's powdered cheek when they left.
Then they walked half a block and her aunt
dropped dead on the sidewalk.

How close does the dragon's spume
have to come? How wide does the crack
in heaven have to split?
What would people look like
if we could see them as they are,
soaked in honey, stung and swollen,
reckless, pinned against time?

from The Human Line
(Copper Canyon Press, 2007)

" All I know for sure is that I
had a hunger for this kind of
meaningful communication—
and I still do."

Larry Robinson

The first time I really "got" poetry was hearing a friend recite Rilke's Archaic Torso Of Apollo. It changed my life!

In high school and college I had read the requisite great poems and learned how to analyze and scan them for rhythm and rhyme and symbol and style. And, of course, they stayed in my head, as did I.

But then I heard a poem that had been taken into the body, made part of it and brought back out into speech. It was immediately apprehensible and awakened in me something that had been asleep for longer than I could remember.

I began to listen in a new way and to read poetry to myself out loud rather than just silently off the page. This inspired me to begin memorizing a few good poems. I discovered that the poems that I took into my own body went to work on me in a profound way, like medicine or a zen koan.

I am now inhabited by about 200 poems which continue to enrich my inner life. Several times a year I host poetry salons whose only rule is "no reading". People are encouraged to bring poems, stories and songs learned by heart. It is not a performance or a competition or a slam. Rather, what emerges over the course of the evening is a kind of poetic conversation that feeds the soul.

This practice has fed my own writing of poetry. I have no interest in academic rules of poetry or in literary criticism. They certainly have their places, just not in my life. What matters to me in the poetry I write and the poetry I imbibe is how it feels on the tongue and in the body and whether it connects me with something greater than myself.

Rumi advises us to "start a large, foolish project - like Noah." My large, foolish project is to restore the soul of the world through restoring the oral tradition of poetry.

Roll Away The Stone

This fecund earth has lain covered long
enough.
It wants to throw off its asphalt blankets,
Stretch and yawn and send forth
Ten thousand blades of grass.

Behind their dams, rivers dream of the sea.
They yearn to burst their bonds and run wild,
To feel the caress of the banks and beyond,
To sing their ancient songs of joy and aban-
don.

Something has been calling to you
For longer than you can remember.
Calling you to step out into the light, into
your life.
It doesn't matter whether you think you're
ready or not.
The time has come.
Roll away the stone!
Roll away the stone!

❝ I discovered that the poems
that I took into my own body
went to work on me in a
profound way, like medicine or
a zen koan."

Jay Leeming

What brought me to poetry were the joys of the imagination, but a love of the music of words soon followed. As a child I was often inspired to dream up alternatives to my daily reality; words are a good way to express those alternatives, those thoughts running like a river just below the corridor of days and hours. I also spent many years as a songwriter, so that has nourished my love of poetry in many indirect ways. Writing words to be sung aloud was a great education in sound. As an adult, imagination can be not simply a way to escape but a way to give back to the community. I have enjoyed the completion of that circle very much, and the push-pull dialogue between what is and what isn't, what stays in place and what scampers away like a coyote to smell out new possibilities.

Grandpa Putting Salt on his Ice Cream

He would hold the salt shaker
in his right hand, and tap the end
over the dark chocolate.
"It enhances the flavor," he would say.
He had more ice cream in his life
than his ancestors ever did, and more butter,
and more milk, and more eggs.
And when these things filled his veins
and pulled him down,
when the barn of his heart caught fire,
it was those ancestors that his eyes
rolled back to see;
strong Norwegian brothers
driving their cows out of the fields
towards the market and the city,
towards railroads and electric lights,
towards world wars and cameras,
towards his body, his thoughts
and his life.

" what stays in place and what scampers away like a coyote to smell out new possibilities."

Greg Kimura

How I Came to Poetry

I never liked poetry. As a writer I mocked it as the effete effeminate impoverished literary step-sister of novels, plays, short stories and screenplays. As a reader, I didn't understand it. Then, halfway through life, chewed up and with all the flavor and juice sucked out of me like a used tobacco wad, I found myself spit out in the middle of a forested retreat center called Loon Lake in Canada. It was there I found poetry.

I spent the first half of my life answering the unspoken question yoked to all men of my age: Can you make a place in the world, expand your kingdom, and extend your lineage? I focused all my decisions and energy in answering "Yes!" I raised two terrific daughters with my excellent wife in a fine house with a great job.

But toward my 40th year, a new question arose. It demanded: Who am I really, and why am I here? The question appeared briefly during my college years, but after graduation, I locked it in the attic with my father's and grandfather's dreams. But fifteen years later, the question began shuffling and scuffing the ceiling. I tried to ignore it, but one day it kicked down the attic door and took up residence in the living room, backyard, office; even the bedroom.

Not long after, I found myself weeping--for the first time in over a decade—in the woods of Vancouver at the Loon Lake Men's Retreat. I often need to get out of my normal life in order to find my truer deeper life. A good men's retreat provides a space for this, as well as fostering all manner of creative confusion and impossible beauty.

Say what you will about a mid-life crisis, but if you don't have one–that's a crisis. The retreat helped me find my soul that had become buried in the basement of my life. The primary tool used was the language of the heart–poetry. For a week I washed in the ecstatic waters of Rumi, of Hafiz; the dark waters of Rilke and Goethe. I washed in the holy waters of William Stafford, Yeats, Neruda and Mary Oliver; of Alison Luterman, Antonio Machado and Luis Rodriguez.

Then, soon after, came my own clumsy attempts to use words to paint images and capture ideas; tentative at first and unbelieving, as if granted permission to enter a holy chamber. Pure foolishness, those first lines, and yet pure spirit. I shared those lines in a room full of men, searching for their own spirit, their own authenticity. Smiles, sighs, laughter, medicine for their wounds and my own.

I came to poetry not because I wanted it, but because I needed it.

_____

Cargo
For Malidoma Some', Loon Lake 2000

You enter life a ship laden with meaning, purpose and gifts
sent to be delivered to a hungry world.
And as much as the world needs your cargo,
you need to give it away.
Everything depends on this.

But world forgets its needs,
and you forget your mission,
and the ancestral maps used to guide you
have become faded scrawls on the parchment of
dead Pharaohs.
The cargo weighs you heavy the longer it is held
and spoilage becomes a risk.
The ship sputters from port to port and at each
you ask:
"Is this the way?"
But the way cannot be found without knowing
the cargo,
and the cargo cannot be known without
recognizing there is a way,
and it is simply this:
You have gifts.
The world needs your gifts.
You must deliver them.

The world may not know it is starving,
but the hungry know,
and they will find you
when you discover your cargo
and start to give it away.

" … my own clumsy attempts to use words to paint images and capture ideas; tentative at first and unbelieving, as if granted permission to enter a holy chamber."

Marge Saiser

How Poetry Came To Me

I signed up. Seemed like a good idea: poet will come to your classroom, write a poem with your fourth graders, and get them to write poems of their own. So the poet came, Bill Kloefkorn, wearing his cotton shirt and blue jeans and soft brown shoes. Kansas boy in his voice. It was the voice. It was how he played with words on the chalkboard. I wrote the assignment along with the kids. I was hooked. My poem turned out to be about snorkeling, which I had done once in my life, scared to pieces. I ended the poem with the line "afraid I will fail."

The poet read my poem, chewed on his Number 2 pencil, and added a line:

afraid I will fail,
afraid I might yet succeed.

Wow, I thought, so poetry knows me. I signed up for poetry courses at the university, paid my money, went to class, read at open mics. The power of the word. Like painting with oils, but no turpentine, no rags. Well, OK, some sticky spots, namely groups where someone who has not written a poem for months wants to take yours and beat the bejesus out of it. But that's life.

Alan Ginsberg came through my city and did a reading. An old man, an old mystery in the auditorium, every face turned to the poet, words washing over us. I thought: Look at what I've been missing.

I wrote my poems on Saturday mornings, riding on the exquisite feeling of two whole days without going to the job. I found I loved revising. Early Monday morning I printed out my most recent version and slipped the paper under Bill Kloefkorn's office door on my way to work. In Wednesday's mail, I got the poem back with Bill's chicken scratches on it. I wanted to learn what I could do with language because the chicken scratches seemed to say "Kick it up a notch." He gave me assignments: write a poem with a 50-word title; make it about water. I would write a 35-word title and a poem about stones. I like that about poetry. When it gets going, it is a stream running downhill and you don't tell it where to go.

I began to buy poetry books, sometimes reading poems aloud to myself in my garret/living room. I purchased Bill's books. Ah, so the stuff of life was the stuff of poetry. Poetry seemed to tell me that the ordinary life is important. The ordinary life counts. And the details! One poem gathered me up in its two paws and growled down into my face a detail about air filling curtains. In the poem, two lovers had had a fight—I knew the fight was supposed to be the main thing --but for me it was that river of air entering at midnight, billowing the curtains like sails, pouring over the sill into the room, poetry coming to me.

———————————————

Pulling Up Beside My Husband At The Stoplight

We are going to the same place
but we take two cars.
Sunday morning
and there's not much traffic
so I pull up beside him at the stoplight.

There he is in his car, beside my car,
his silhouette in the window,
the brown of his hair against his neck.
He turns and blows me a kiss. I watch it
float on by. I ask for another.

I remember how he comes into the dark bedroom
early on the weekday mornings,
the sound of his workboots across the carpet,
the scent of his face when he finds me in the covers,
kisses my eyebrow
and the corner of my mouth,
tells me the weather report
and the precise time of day.

So I roll down the window,
whistle in my throat, do my best baboon snorting,
pull my glasses crooked on my face,
pound the horn as if it were bread dough.
There is only the lady in the white Buick,
but he is embarrassed,
glad to see the green.
Me, I'm stepping on the gas,
catching up,
wondering what I can do at 56th and Calvert.

"I like that about poetry. When it gets going, it is a stream running downhill and you don't tell it where to go."

96

Wendy McVicker

Poetry Bliss

Where does it come from? As a small child I was comforted rocking on a parent's lap in the white–painted chair, listening to stories or songs. My father read, my mother sang, the chair creaked; all blurred and blended, phrases from stories and nursery rhymes and songs weaving together in a rich tissue of sound and imagery and sheer physical pleasure. Wynken, Blynken and Nod one night sailed off in their wooden shoe, and oh! to go down to the sea again, in the Owl's and the Pussycat's pea green boat—the escape envisioned here not away from reality, but toward a deeper reality, the reality plumbed by the imagination with the tools of language and song: poetry. Later I would encounter "Suddenly I realize/That if I stepped out of my body I would break/ Into blossom." and be thrilled by the naming of what I had only sensed, and wondered about, hardly daring to name it myself.

A child of words and dreaming, I first tried sorting out the world with the mind's keen tools of discursive language and linear narrative. But the body would not be denied, its need for movement, its desire for pattern and rhythm. It wasn't until I realized that poetry combined (or could combine) intellectual delight with visceral pleasure that I found the medium I needed to understand and articulate my world. Here was the satisfaction of words, story, images, allied with sound and rhythm: the beating heart and the tales that it tells. Now my journey could begin.

And I'm traveling still—

Where do they go?

When the dead leave us,
where do they go?
Are they lolling on clouds,
watching us weep as they play
instruments they never touched
in this life?
Are they wandering
in murk and mist, howling?
Have they crossed
the black river, forgotten
our names?

Is that his voice I hear

when the geese fly over
in September?
Has the blue of her eyes
entered this stone, this shimmer
at the edge of the sea, the blue
jay's feather?
And that cool touch I feel
at dusk on the trail
by the water—?

What is forever,
if not this moment,
when I turn toward you
in the warmth of our bed,
and feel your pulse
echoing my own?

" It wasn't until I realized that poetry combined (or could combine) intellectual delight with visceral pleasure that I found the medium I needed to understand and articulate my world."

Dorianne Laux

I have recently begun to think of writing as what Susan Sontag calls "a wisdom project" in her forward to *Another Beauty*, a collection of autobiographical essays by the great Polish poet Adam Zagajewski.

"...autobiography is an occasion to purge oneself of vanity, while advancing the project of self understanding—call it the wisdom project—which is never completed, however long the life."

I am still hard at work on this project of the self. The solitary self, as well as the self in relation to the world and the unknown universe we swirl around in, uncertain of our purpose or future. When I wrote the poems that would become my first book, I didn't think of it as a book, but rather as a need to understand the basic questions that all human beings ask: Who am I? Why am I here? Where am I going? What is beauty? Why is there suffering? Where is truth? These questions would arise in me in the form of poems, and in making the poems into a collection, I tried to arrange them in a shape, find a path for them to travel to make clearer those questions. I write to know the questions.

Poem after poem, book after book, the ante is upped. I think this could be why it takes so long between books. The poet is working harder each time to go deeper, farther, layering on or stripping away to find the exact color or texture, the core or the root, the frail light or the watery dark. I write to work things out. I write to concentrate, to feel a sense of purpose rise up in me. I enjoy the struggle of making a new object to present to the world, a gift made from scratch—whole, unique, edible as bread. And I want that gift to travel well, packed into an old boat on calm water or hidden inside a greased body diving into a blue pool, a sleek arrow that leaves a feathered silence and wonder in its wake. I like moving, word by word, toward a sense of discovery, toward an awareness of self-- a curious, energetic, intelligent, sacred, baffling, depthful, heartful self. I work to find my subject, something I can sink my teeth into. I live for that flaring up of language, when the words actually carry me, envelope me, grip me. And all the above is why I read poetry, to hear the truth, spoken harshly or whispered into my ear, to see more clearly the world's beauty and sadness, to be lifted up and torn down, to be remade, by language, to become larger, swollen with life.

I write to add my voice to the sum of voices, to be part of the choir. I write to be one sequin among the shimmering others, hanging by a thread from the evening gown of the world. I write to remember. I write to forget myself, to be so completely immersed in the will of the poem that when I look up from the page I can still smell the smoke from the house burning in my brain. I write to destroy the blank page, unravel the ink, use up what I've been given and give it away. I write to make the trees shiver at the sliver of sun slipping down the axe blade's silver lip. I write to hurt myself again, to dip my fingertip into the encrusted pool of the wound. I write to become someone else, that better, smarter self that lives inside my dumbstruck twin. I write to invite the voices in, to watch the angel wrestle, to feel the devil gather on its haunches and rise. I write to hear myself breathing. I write to be doing something while I wait to be called to my appointment with death. I write to be done writing. I write because writing is fun.

Dark Charms

Eventually the future shows up everywhere:
the burly summers and unslept nights
in deep lines and dark splotches, thinning skin.
Here is the corner store grown to a condo,
the bike reduced to one spinning wheel,
the ghost of a dog that used to be, her trail
no longer trodden, just a dip in the weeds.
The clear water we drank as thirsty children
still runs through our veins. Stars we saw then
we still see now, only fewer, dimmer, less often.
The old tunes play and continue to move us
in spite of our learning, the wraith of romance,
lost innocence, literature, the death of the poets.
We continue to speak, if only in whispers,
to something inside us that longs to be named.
We name it the past and drag it behind us,
bag like a lung filled with shadow and song,
dreams of running, the keys to lost names.

" I write to be one sequin among the shimmering others, hanging by a thread from the evening gown of the world."

Marissa McNamara

Why I Write Poetry

I am five years old. It is 6:30am, still cool and muggy, and I pad quietly past my mother's room. She would send me back to bed saying, "It's too early. Go back to sleep." She could not imagine this time as part of her waking day. In the kitchen my grandmother smokes a cigarette. Too early for this one to have the thick pink ring of lipstick on its filter. She wears a blue and white checked housecoat. She grabs a basket and we go outside where the light is just lifting in mist from the pond behind her house. Sound is muffled and soft. Quiet. Side by side, we pick green beans from the poles in the garden and place them in her basket. At my grandmother's house, there is earth and what rises from it, and there is the morning to lead us into the day.

Poetry takes vigilance. The poet must be alert and aware; she must listen anew to everyday sounds like the sawing of a gloved woman scraping ice from her windshield on a January morning, the echo it makes from the street to the bedroom window. To be a poet, you must notice the metal taste of water from a hose. You have to pay attention, to pause and appreciate. You have to notice and remember, a constant pen in hand, and live as one who must let go of everything while simultaneously opening the heart to memory. You must take the time to be entranced by the little things, by the smell of a freshly unwrapped bar of your grandmother's soap or the way the crickets sound on a summer night.

And then as a writer you want to take those images and offer them to others and ask, Here—do you remember these things too? Because you want to share in that something that lives in each heart, to connect to the heart that knows when it hears truth—the taste of the metal water not just the taste but the feeling of summer, of freedom, the way the world felt in the spaces between May and September.

Human beings hunger for connection. Poets try to link us together through words and images. If we're lucky, we can reach out to the reader's heart. And if we're really, really lucky, the reader will nudge the person next to him, maybe someone in the bookstore, a stranger or a lover, maybe, and say, Here—read this, and the person will, and she will smile too and nod, and they will have entered that moment together and, if only briefly, recognize that they are not such separate beings.

A good poem can hold your hand; a great poem will ask you to reach out and hold someone else's.

Mother of Us All

When Eve offered her fruit to Adam,
said, Give this a try,
and he did, and they were banished,
they couldn't blame her mother.

There was no Mrs. Eve
on the other end of that rib,
no evil matriarch whose profile
haunted Eve in the mirror,
no woman who'd told her she was dirty,
beaten her with a wooden spoon.

There was no obsessive compulsive
abusive narcissistic protective overbearing
yet emotionally unavailable mother
who stifled Eve's self esteem
such that she couldn't say no to a serpent
because he might not like her
because, in her heart, she wanted to be loved
so much that she took up with a snake
and lured Adam in too because, of course,
her legacy was to be overbearing and with-holding too,
and Adam knew if he didn't give in,
she'd be passive aggressive, smile in his face
and piss in his coffee, so he took her fruit and ate it.

Poor Eve. It would be so much easier
if only she'd had a mother to blame.

" A good poem can hold your
hand; a great poem will ask
you to reach out and hold
someone else's."

Naomi Shihab Nye

As a small child, listening to poems read at bedtime by my mother before I could read for myself—Emily Dickinson, Robert Louis Stevenson, Langston Hughes—I felt the calm of well-chosen sentences overtake me.

Poems didn't argue.
Poems didn't say too much. They honored the listener—beautiful small muffins or biscuits of words, extended on a plate. There it is.
Poems respected details and connected them in unusual ways.
Poems made the world slow down—that deep savoring and sensation of a held moment.
I think now—poems also clear the air.

So the first thing I wanted to do, upon learning to write in first grade, was write some myself. It always felt possible.

Naomi Shihab Nye
FROM, YOU & YOURS
(BOA EDITIONS, 2007)

Jerusalem

"Let's be the same wound if we must bleed.
Let's fight side by side, even if the enemy
is ourselves: I am yours, you are mine."
-Tommy Olofsson, Sweden

I'm not interested in
Who suffered the most.
I'm interested in
people getting over it.

Once when my father was a boy
a stone hit him on the head.
Hair would never grow there.
Our fingers found the tender spot
and its riddle: the boy who has fallen
stands up. A bucket of pears
in his mother's doorway welcomes him home.
The pears are not crying.
Later his friend who threw the stone
says he was aiming at a bird.
And my father starts growing wings.

Each carries a tender spot:
something our lives forgot to give us.
A man builds a house and says,
"I am native now."
A woman speaks to a tree in place
of her son. And olives come.
A child's poem says,
"I don't like wars,
they end up with monuments."

He's painting a bird with wings
wide enough to cover two roofs at once.

Why are we so monumentally slow?
Soldiers stalk a pharmacy:
big guns, little pills.
If you tilt your head just slightly
it's ridiculous.

There's a place in my brain
Where hate won't grow.
I touch its riddle: wind, and seeds.
Something pokes us as we sleep.

It's late but everything comes next.

Photographer | **Michael Nye**

" Poems didn't argue.
Poems didn't say too much.
They honored the listener
- beautiful small muffins or
biscuits of words, extended
on a plate."

Luis Rodriguez

Poetry came to me in torrents, when I least expected it, when I was in a crossroads, most lost, most unclear. I was a heroin addict, in a violent gang, but also trying to move away from this life—painting murals, becoming a Chicano activist & revolutionary thinker, writing.

I ended up in Berkeley, age 18, just released from jail, having lost twenty five of my friends to "La Vida Loca," and straddling the fence of living or dying. Friends there invited me to my first poetry reading—with then master poets Jose Montoya, David Henderson, and Pedro Pietri. They were Chicano, African American and Puerto Rican. They were the OGs of street poetry, pulling from the depths of lives similar to mine, but making blossoms and bullets out of every line.

When they read poetry this knocked me off my feet. I had never heard words spoken this way. More music than talk. More fevered shapes than sentences. More Che and Malcolm than Shakespeare. They instigated a rebellion in my chest; they gave me an ear for the poetic image, sound, sensation. Prior to this I had written lines myself: vignettes, ideas, emotions. I didn't know they were poems. I had no idea what a poem was. Finally, at this reading, I woke up to my own stories, my own voice, the powerful energy that would eventually allow poetry to spring forth, to live on the stage and the page.

Now, thirty-five years later, I live and breathe poetry. I have written many books, started a poetry press, and opened a multi-arts cultural space and bookstore called Tia Chucha's Centro Cultural in our barrio community of the Northeast San Fernando Valley.

That moment in 1973, when I first heard poetry, proved to be quite an ignition, a hell of a combustion, that exploded over the years into these books, the press, this cultural space. In hard economic times like now, when most people and institutions tend to push away the arts and creative endeavor, this is precisely when we need more poetry, more art, more imaginative lives.

Until we have poetry at the center of the culture again, our country will remain unjust, ambiguous, lost, and superficial. The fact of the matter is poetry in the United States is the most powerful and influential in the world, even at the margins. Instead of beating at the periphery, it needs to beat at the center.

Moonlight to Water Luis J. Rodriguez
(For my youngest sons, Ruben and Luis)

Ruben recalled the day I brought mama
and his baby brother home when he was six.
In the back seat of the car, he said,
was an Asian looking child,
hair sticking straight up on his head.

Chito—short for Luisito—looked this way
because he's part *Raramuri* and *Huichol*,
but mostly all universe.
Ruben must have wondered about the
    galaxy of stars,
bird songs and stories that had been dreamt
to fashion such a boy.

When Chito arrived I'm sure Ruben knew
—his world would never be the same.

Until then, Ruben had been our only child.
To mom and dad, he was the screech
of car brakes,
a sigh to a bad joke,
the glove to our ball,
and now this—a bewildered boy gazing
at a sweet-faced earth child
wrapped in a light-blue blanket.

I asked Ruben what he thought about his brother.
Eyes gleaming with a six-year-old's clarity,
he answered: "Oh, I already knew him
—I saw Chito when I was in mama's stomach."

I gave Ruben a look I often offered
in reply to his amazing observations.
Somehow, though, the statement rang true.
His younger brother was in the wings,
preparing to part, the next one,
patiently abiding his turn.

As they grew older, Chito followed his brother's
every move, entering wide-eyed
into Ruben's dense sphere,
sharing the same music, games, imaginings.

Ruben never hurt or exploited him,
as older brothers often do.

The boys connected from the start,
like hummingbird to flower,
like poems to breath,
like moonlight to water,
brothers since the womb.

"Finally, at this reading, I woke up to my own stories, my own voice, the powerful energy that would eventually allow poetry to spring forth, to live on the stage and the page."

106

Lisa Starr

My Call to Poetry, or Poetry's Call to Me

"Why speak of the use of poetry?
Poetry is what uses us."
—Hayden Carruth

I never really chose to be a poet, nor was it one teacher or mentor or writer that first called me specifically to poetic expression. Rather, poetry chose me. A self-taught reader by the age of three, I'm told, I loved reading and writing in all of its shapes and sizes. I was precocious, creative, and hyperactive in school, and fortunately, a few significant elementary school teachers, early on, encouraged me to turn my "exuberance for life" into writing of my own.

Then, when I was 11, the writing of poetry went from being classroom distraction to necessity, for that was the year my father, an almost straight from *To Kill a Mock-ingbird* kind of small town hero got sick and began to die slowly, at home. Like Atticus Finch, my father was both an attorney and a champion communicator who urged us, who urged everyone, to use language to try to make the world a better place.

My mother, in many ways my father's opposite, suffered horribly from depression, so communicating, like most things, was a tremendous burden to her. And so I turned to language, to writing as a way to learn the truth, since no one in my world seemed prepared or equipped to speak it themselves, and thus it was that through poems I first taught myself not only that my father probably wasn't ever going to get better, but also that we would all somehow get through it. I used poems as a route to the largely unsaid story of my own heart, and the hearts of those I cared most about—my parents, my siblings, my animals. I wrote poems as a method of navigating this living, and here's the secret: I still do.

I write because the joys and the sorrows and the daily dozen indignities and graces alike deserve their place in the light. I write because we live in a culture where people are embarrassed about whom and what they love, what they grieve, and what adds meaning and texture to their lives. I write because I saw a young woman I know in the store yesterday whom I haven't seen in two months—not since I read in the paper about the crib death of her three-month-old baby girl, Ava. I write because when I said "Oh sweetheart, how are you?" she said, brave voice wavering, "I'm doing fine. We're all do-ing (deep breath) just fine."

I don't know many people who are "doing just fine." I'd like to know what they look like, and talk about, and order in restaurants. I'd like to know how they get through the first few days after one's beloved pet dies. Or one's mother. Meantime, I just try to get through it by writing. Writing through the whole blessed mess of it. Language for me is the thing that reconnects me to life and to the people I've been blessed (and challenged) to share it with. And so as life keeps happening to me the way it seems to for most of us—relationship, career, family, loss, work, change—it is writing that remains my most constant companion.

So whatever it is that calls me to the gladness of living—and the grief of it too—that is what first, and still, calls me to poetry. The poems come when they will, but usually, as with most things, all at once or not at all. More than anything else, the writing of poems requires a certain quality of being present with and in the world, as if all of it matters, exactly as it is. When we allow our-selves to experience life in this way then everything, even the blunders, and perhaps them most of all, becomes sacred business. Sacred and silly. So writing poems then, is about constantly being surprised and delighted by this busy, old world, and the simple act of it, of taking this sometimes blazing hand to paper, filling me with a simultaneous sense of wonder and worthiness—a sense that I am somehow doing my work—of doing my part in the world, as Marge Piercy said, "to be of use."

In The End
For Eliot, September 7, 2004

And after everything, what is there to
say, really,
to an animal whose death
one has long been expecting?
Perhaps it's best not to say anything.
Better just to sit with him—
to stroke the fur that no one's washed
in months,
to scratch the ears which no longer
hear,
to slowly shift that golden flop of a
friend
to the spot he'd loved the best:
a little hilltop overlooking a harbor
where the boats are forever turning
toward the morning light,
where the heron is always just now
landing, its ripple a whisper.

And careful with the legs, which
stopped working, forever,
sometime last night, you turn him
around gently
so that even though he can't see so
well his body can remember.
And that's when he raises his fine
head just one more time
to honor this slender, splendid patch
of life—
the geese flying high and North
forever,
the boats with their delicate dance.
He holds his head that way for several
minutes though it hurts—
one more time smelling what's West,
and the breeze dallies one final time
in the soft fur of his chest.

And that's when you whisper, though
you're weeping
"It will be okay, it will be okay."
And he shifts a thick, gentle paw, and
somehow it finds your hand.
And may you have the sense, then, to
sit with him in silence,
and to understand what he's been

saying all along—
to know, at last, what it means to
love the earth this way—
to endure this kind of pain
just for one more morning's breeze,
and the boats, and the blue,
so much blue.

“ More than anything else,
the writing of poems
requires a certain quality
of being present with and
in the world, as if all of it
matters, exactly as it is.”

Pilgrimage to the Temple of Words

Presented for Power of Poetry 2009 by Alan Cohen

In his book Danger on Peaks, the poet, Gary Snyder, steeped in Asian culture and thoughts shares an email received immediately after the Taliban destroyed the giant Buddhas at the edge of the Bamiyan Valley in Afghanistan. The writer seems to find comfort in the idea that eventually, everything "…will decay."

Snyder reminds us that everything "…will decay" is only part of the story. He adds: "Ah yes…impermanence. But this is never a reason to let compassion and focus slide, or to pass off the suffering of others because they are merely impermanent beings."

He goes on to quote a haiku by Issa:

Tsuyu no yo wa
Tsuyu no ya nagara
Sarinagara

This dewdrop world
Is but a dewdrop world
And yet—

Snyder suggests that "and yet— " become our permanent practice, embracing our personal spark of compassion and focus in the ever flowing sea of impermanence.

*****

The everyday English we use to navigate the world seems to work fairly well. We can give and get directions and use such language to order products, follow recipes, describe architecture, and debate sports and politics.

It is, however, limited when we attempt to hold two seemingly contradictory ideas simultaneously, or to realize that various concepts — education, marriage, peace — are ongoing processes rather than immutably fixed concrete ideas. We get into the same old arguments that something must be either good or bad, black or white. We are disappointed again and again when we get to a peaceful resolution of a conflict, and then the amity does not last. These are times when our language works like a one-way trap.

This is the Chinese character for poetry. It is a composite made of the characters "words" and "temple". Poetry is a temple for words. A temple is the place to open oneself to the experience of our connection to a wider world, universe, or way of thinking and being. One's actions and speech in a temple deserve to be undertaken with care and intention. When we truly desire connection with something greater than ourselves alone, it is necessary to act with such care and intention —the essence of the behavior we call, "caressing"— and to make this behavior a part of ourselves, whether inside the temple or outside of it.

It has been suggested that the Japanese language, built on the sound of vowels, connected to the breath of the cosmos, mirrors the natural world In Sanskrit, the word for the sound of the universe "aum", is a fully released breath.

Languages like English, deriving, as they do, from German, (originally the Norse – sounds of the North, the cold, limited light, people), are thick with consonants, which stop the breath by shaping the mouth to craft particular sounds.

Is it possible that at such a basic level of thought and feeling, the shaping of our mouth and tongue to produce consonants causes our thought process to constantly stop and start, by our breath being forced to contract and release abruptly through the doors of the mouth as language travels into the world?

Again, that haiku from Issa:

Tsuyu no yo wa
Tsuyu no ya nagara
Sarinagara

This dewdrop world
Is but a dewdrop world
And yet—

The Japanese, even if we don't understand it, flows easily. The English version has a much harder feel even when we understand the ethereal concept of the dewdrop world. This poetic rendition is superior to an explanation because it imitates motion, fluidity, an aspect of the universal that stirs the otherwise inanimate, the concrete, into motion.

The Japanese haiku form compresses these words to the essence of a profound idea, thus pulling us out of conventional thought patterns. When we live a life that includes occasional pilgrimages to a word temple it becomes necessary that we speak poetically, which literally derives from the root meaning "to create".

By embracing this realization it becomes possible to envision continuums rather than diametrical opposites when we think. As the yin/yang, symbol (originally the Chinese Tai Chi ("tai" way, + manner, "chi", animating energy, i.e. the manner by which energy moves –the Grand Ultimate) demonstrates, white and black define each other, a small dot of each within the other. There is no North without South, or day without night. The word temple holds all varying degrees of everything. As related by Ikkyu, an ancient rascally Zen priest:

I'd love to give you something
but, what would help?
Self other right wrong
wasting your life arguing
face it
you're happy, really
you are happy.

The world and everything in it is an ongoing process. Once we are trapped in the uncertainty principle of modern physics of either focusing on the speed or location of a particle by specifying one particle in isolation, the other is lost. However when we look at one particle, while realizing that we are just seeing one aspect of it rather than the entire physical condition in which it exists, we can remember, not forget, that we are a process too, ever changing in many ways.

Institutions like peace, relationships or marriage are not stable entities. They are more like someone standing on an acrobat's bongo board, a short plank poised on a cylinder. Standing stably on the plank pressed against the moving cylinder requires mastering the art of balance, which derives from realizing that a permanent static point does not exist. Stability requires a constant series of adjustments and corrections about a center. It takes effort and discipline to maintain ones equilibrium, but with practice, achieving balance while in motion becomes second nature. As Theodore Roethke says, "This shaking keeps me steady. I should know."

The temple is always open. We can find our path to it through practicing the poetic voice when we desire to live more fully in this dewdrop world.

The Erlking

Presented for The Power of Poetry 2009 by Alan Cohen
(German poem: Goethe, English translation and new music: Dolce)

Who rides so late through the windy night?
It's a father with a child;
He holds his son in his arms,
To keep the boy so close and warm.
"My son, why hide your face in fear?"
Father, don't you see the Erlking?
The Erlking's Crown and flowing Robe?
"My son, it's just a wisp of fog."
"O, you dear child, come along with me!
Such a lovely game we'll play!
Fragrant flowers the shores abound,
My mother's made you a Golden Gown ."
Father, father, do you not hear
What the Erlking has promised me ?
"Be quiet, my child, be still;
'Tis but the dry leaves rustling."
"Won't you come along with me, fine boy?
My girls will tend your keeping.
The Daughters dance such lullabies,
'Twill sing you off to sleeping."
O father, father, why can't you see
The Erlking's daughters dark and gay?
"My son, my son, there's no one there
But Willow trees twisted and grey."
"I love you, boy; your charming face;
But if you're not willing, then I'll use force."
Father, father, he's grabbing me!
The Erlking is hurting me!
The father shudders and rides so fast,
He holds his moaning child.
To the courtyard swiftly his horse has sped,
But in his arms . . . the child was dead.

The Erlking is the ruler of the Other World, the place of dreams, poems, and artistic vision. Where everything is like this world, but much more so. The language of this place is metaphor.

We cannot enter this world at will. Sometimes, against all seeming reason, we suddenly find that we have somehow been carried there. If we consciously want to visit the Other World, we can only make ourselves ready to go, and then look for places where the veil between the worlds is thin, places where we can be amazed, and held in a state of awe. The natural world provides many doorways. If we find a quiet place, quiet our self, and simply open to how the myriad forms of Nature avail their selves to us we may find ourselves there.

Traditionally in wisdom stories and dreams, all characters are aspects of our self. In the song you have just heard, a father rides through life with his son. The son, that younger and more open part of us, notices the Other World, and is drawn to it strongly. It calls to him like it called to all of us when we were children. The father, the grown part of us that has gotten down to business, thrown frivolity aside, who embraces rationality and practicality, creates and imposes proficiency testing on our youth, continues to explain away what his son's senses tell him. He succeeds in killing in his son, the part of him that travels between worlds.

The Erlking is the most striking character in the story. He is the ruler of the other world – the polar opposite of the father. He is the king of song and dream, poetic language and beauty. Scholars think the word Erlking is a mistaken version of Elvenking–king of the elves. In German, erl means alder, a many branched tree that lives in wet places. Tree lore tells us that alder was used for magic wands. It is a wood that is known for protection against drowning and acts as a shield against death curses, ill-omens and destructive emotions. It cultivates visions of inner and outer worlds, helping to bridge above and below.

When holding a piece of alder, we are literally connecting to a part of the natural word that reminds us of the Other World. We are then prepared to go to that place of awe and mystery; wonder and magic. If we pierce the veil and have an experience there, we can upon our return, enter into a state of poesis or creation, and produce a piece of art, thus shaping our lives into a fuller and richer existence. Because alder protects us from drowning, we can pull back to our everyday world and chop wood, carry water, pay the bills and sustain ourselves until the next visit to the Other World. We should not choose one world or the other, but travel between them in as conscious a way as we are able to do.

In the Arthurian romances, all of the knights enter the forest at their own place to search for the Grail, that which feeds them. We too can make this choice, to enter into the natural world to find where the boundary is thin, and like Sir Percival, whose name literally means to pierce the veil, find that which we need to nourish our deeper lives.

> The breeze at dawn has secrets to tell you
> Don't go back to sleep.
> You must ask what you really want.
> Don't go back to sleep.
> People are going back and forth across the doorsill
> Where the two worlds touch.
> The door is round and open.
> Don't go back to sleep.

Rumi
Coleman Barks translation

Power of Poetry 2006

The following are four reflections, from the four principal presenters, of the Power of Poetry Festival. This festival was held in Logan, Ohio in April of 2006.

This presentation gives a window into a community event, one which provided that most American invention, practical and useable tools, for people to rescue their lives from the emotional constraints of physical imprisonment and the numbing effects of daily life
in our culture.

It is a model of what anyone can create in their community, given they are willing to exert the effort to bring life back to themselves and
others in a creative, joyful way; for a renewed sense of life.

The presenters wrote their reflections after the event, and did not discuss what they wrote with each other beforehand. You, the reader, have a fresh, unedited, view of the Power of Poetry brought into the lives of an ordinary community in mid-America, in two different environments, a prison environment and main street U.S.A.

In an entertainment age of canned experiences and televised "reality TV" this is a fresh, un-rehearsed view of what is still possible when people who care enough create a simple cultural event which does much more than entertain, more than salve wounds —it resuscitates lives.

We hope you enjoy what we have devoted our efforts to produce.
Why not try it for yourself?

Captivess and Poetry: The Power of Poetry Festival
Walking the Road of Beauty
April 2006
Logan, Ohio
Organized by Alan Cohen
Musical performance: Evie Adelman
Invited poets: Greg Kimura
Mel S. Kimura Bucholtz
I sit in the Logan Hocking County Library, an

oasis in the lush but impoverished hills of southeast Ohio. My wife next to me, her fingers tingling with the piano notes of the Schubert lieder she has just finished playing. At the front of the room Mel is at the podium, warming up the crowd with the words of Antonio Machado:

"…wanderer, there is no path, the path is made by walking. By walking one makes the road, and upon glancing behind one sees the path that never will be trod again."

I close my eyes seeing the road behind me that has led to this moment, stretching back along a forest path; dogwood petals spaced like Hansel's bread crumbs, intensely green trees dripping with the springtime rain.

There are a lineage of poets who've come here in the past four years. Each year the audience has grown and the poetry festival seemed like a good idea rather than an impossibility.

The poet, Luis Rodriguez, stands beside a redwood in the mist, throwing out the challenge to a hundred men at a conference in California to put more poetry, thus beauty, into the world. I feel that Luis is talking directly to me.

Mel appears again, at workshop long ago, spinning Roethke's mysterious trace, *"I wake to sleep…"* A long shut gate has opened for me into the poetic world.

Wanda Bowers, sophomore English martinet, feared by all, writes Pound's lines on the blackboard:

*"The apparition of faces in the crowd,
Petals on a wet black bough."*

I understand the metaphor, realizing most of the class doesn't. Metaphorical thinking connects me to something deeper and secret inside me. But it's not 'cool' for a fourteen year old to go to this place, much less talk about it with my jock friends. So I lock the gate. I hide the key from myself.

Gramps is reading to me. The tone is playful and words sound similar to each other. "They rhyme", he says.

Robert Frost said that one of the things poetry does is "take you to a place you've been to before and thought you'd never return to."

My eyes open. I'm back at the fifth annual Hocking County Festival of Poetry, sitting in a room filled with small town citizens, happy to be here. Two poets stand before us, ready to read their poems and play off of each other's words; like jazz musicians taking each other to a place neither one can get to alone.

The fantasy writer Cyril Block, in his story The Music Spies, describes fugitive musicians secretly ushered into rooms of people waiting to hear them. His story is similar to that of the mission you are going to read about.

In Block's story a time occurred where societies all over were mechanical copies of one another, with variations of language and geography. Their major pastime was consumerism and a civilized slothful lifestyle of being served by machines and services which anesthetized the people, resulting in rampant obesity, an increasing pandemic loss of sensual acuity, eyes began to fail commonly in early thirties, hearing became muffled, audible speech degenerated to hoarse whispers, the skin became parchment -like, major hair loss was common early in life, muscular dexterity atrophied and people shuffled around rather than walking with gusto. Competitive sports became a museum artifact.

The natural landscape was encased in a vast honeycomb of transparent bubbles, humidified like vegetables for sale. The landscape was observed from above by children studying it as greenhouse projects and visited by adults on "fly over" observation vacations. Traditional art objects, once displayed in museums, were digitally reproduced and studied via microchip implant technology; chips inserted in the head by rental subscription. Once inserted, as with other forms of knowledge, pharmaceuticals were taken, drugs which allowed the brain to biochemically "install" knowledge in the structure of the neural net at the cellular level. This made the tedious tasks of curiosity and study things of the past.

Typical of fantasy fiction genre, an underground of people longing for the old days of vitality and sensual beauty emerged in secret around the world. Naturally

anyone suspected of these interests were detained and reprogrammed by neuronal implants and group training.

Despite the efforts of the Government for Containment, Sensory Control for The Betterment of Society (CSCBS) connections were made between disparate groups sharing a common interest in the Re-vitalization of Human Life through Sensation and Imagination (RHLSI).

In Block's world this re-vitalization effort was conducted by music spies, a devoted group of musicians who memorized major pieces of the old music and were either skilled singers, much like the minstrels and Minnesingers of 13/14th Century Europe, or versatile performers on old instruments, in particular the cello, harp, or flute -those instruments which reflected the greatest range of human emotions and/or reflected the emotional range of the human voice.

A typical example of their activity went like this: after careful screening and a trial meeting, designed to eliminate possible traitors, the musician was brought in under cover of darkness to a secret meeting place. He or she was carefully ushered into a meeting room with good acoustic properties, where a group of rigorously screened participants were waiting.

The screeners were master hypnotherapists, men for women, women for men, who could detect by the sound of the voice, syntax, imagery and body gestures, the authenticity of the members.

The meeting would start this way: a mild hypnotic induction would be performed to bring the audience into their best state of receptivity. A list of selections was prepared in advance and the performance began.

The musician would either perform the piece vocally, or by instrument, while the audience was invited to experience the music focusing on their sensations, emotions and imagination.

There often was much crying as people recalled the old experiences of vividly feeling alive once more by the effort of their curious imagination and sensations reawakened once again.

One of my favorite books is a collection of photographs of Japanese gardens. Its title is Islands of Serenity, another poetic indulgence. When I constructed my latest Japanese garden, this title mocked me as I wrenched my muscles, smashed my fingers, and ripped my nails. The poetry would come later. There was hard labor to come first.

The high from the Mosaic conference at Mendocino pushed me onto the path of envisioning a weekend poetry festival. I had the idea. Now all I needed were money, poets, a venue, and an audience.

It may be that when we no longer know what to do
we have come to our real work
and that when we no longer know which way to go
we have begun our real journey.

—Wendell Berry

This event was going to require funding. Artists deserve to be financially recognized for their contributions. The grant road seemed a likely starting point. Thousands of words later, I realized that crafting artistic notions into the dry landscape of grant requirements was impossible. The job became simply deciding what they wanted to hear and giving it to them. My frustration was tempered by friends who generously gave contributions, often despite their own ambivalence to poetry. It felt good to be trusted.

The funding process has been refined over the five years of the festival. We are still soliciting grants, but also asking the public to financially contribute in a small way. Whereas most small town cultural events are sponsored by the same wealthy people, we wanted a more grassroots approach. Individual ownership of the festival was a desirable goal. We used word of mouth and chaining emails to reach out for small contributions. Each solicitation was accompanied by news of the festival and short writings by those who would be involved in presenting the events. These were primarily about a person's realization that poetry was not necessarily the imagination slaying discipline that pedantic teachers had demonstrated. The response was amazing, and $2000 was donated during the first funding campaign.

There have been many moments of doubt. There were many times when I thought the idea of a poetry festival in Logan, Ohio was insane. After a long day of grant writing for the first festival I went to Wal-Mart for cat food. I overheard two ladies in the pet department discussing the merits of new dog outfits for an obese Chihuahua, versus hand-me-downs from

Ol' Fluffy. What was I doing struggling to bring well known poets here to read to these people?

It was almost ridiculous how easy it was to get poets. I had heard one of Alison Luterman's poems, Jesus Incognito, loved it, and called her. When I told her about the festival and invited her to take part she readily agreed. When I told her she was to be paid, she was pleasantly surprised. She had been willing to just do it to spread her words into a wider world. This basic scenario was repeated with others. We have drawn a variety of poets, some well known and some amateurs in the sense that poetry or teaching is not their major source of income. This was done to demonstrate that immersing oneself seriously into the arts was possible and desirable. And that anyone can do this. The audiences loved the 'amateurs' as well as the professionals. I never thought that in Logan, Ohio, people would walk up to me on the street and recite a poem to me, just because they wanted to express themselves in a deeper way than usual.

The members of the community were at first reluctant to attend. Having to pay admission was one of the factors preventing them from coming. Once the festival venue was changed from a school auditorium (schools being the place of numerous bad poetry experiences) to the library, a pleasant space that the public loved, crowds began to grow. The library board began to provide some financial support in order to eliminate the attendance fee. This made it less of a risk to see what the event had to offer. One lady came to the very first reading, brought by a friend. She bought one of Alison's books and stayed up all night reading it. She was hooked. The next year she literally dragged her husband down the street. He looked like a child going to the dentist's office. He heard David Lee's poems, became a big fan, and his foundation became a major financial contributor.

It now looks as if poetry is here to stay in Hocking County, Ohio. People need to be suffused into the arts, whether they know it or not. Once they have felt poetry wash over their minds and burrow into their deepest core, they will not let go of it.

Ins Grüne, ins Grüne, da lockt uns der Früling, der liebliche Knabe, und führt uns am blumenum.
Out into the greenness, out into the greenness, springtime, the lovely boy, beckons us there and leads us, leaning on a staff wound around with flowers.

The words behind the melodic interplay, the piano like the constant dizzying breeze, blowing

petals and fragrance, circling the violin transcribing the words into melody; a direct infusion of green, spring, beauty into the heart. I begin every poetry festival evening with this song by Franz Schubert. This piece makes way for the streams of words to be poured through the variegated green envelope of the Hocking Hills. Music is the gateway, enticing us into the receptive, thirsty part of ourselves that yearns for beauty...silence to sound to music to words...

Schubert lieder are my passions. For years, like an evangelist, I have forced these songs down the ears of any friends who would listen. Immediately after this year's festival a close friend (a devotee of folk, blue-grass, and rock) confessed "I finally fell in love with that first song. I can't get it out of my head." Several weeks later he says the music has left him. I hum the melody and he protests "That won't do any good, without the piano part, it doesn't work." And I know he has "gotten it!"

Performing music has not always been so pleasurable for me. During my time as a music major, and for years after, my limbs would shake uncontrollably, my mind would dissociate while tempos slowed and sped out of control. Years of breath/centering/ grounding work along with the decision only to play music that I really love has helped. Playing duets and chamber music is my vastly preferred mode over solo.

Before the Saturday reading, Mel spun us into a trance (Greg, Alan and I). His "tuning" process relaxed us while heightening sensory aliveness and awareness. But for me the tuning heightened my agitation, the old performance anxiety. I mentioned this problem, entreating Mel to ease this anxiety for me. He proceeded as I remained in the trance. He instructed me to look at my hands, asking "Do they know how to play the music?" I considered the boot camp of practice to which they had been subjected, and also how exciting and how well the final rehearsal had gone. I answered "Yes" with uncharacteristic certainty.

That evening for the first time I had the experience of my hands being alive and wise and happy playing! I felt like their proud parent, helping them shape phrases, reining them in sometimes, but mostly marveling at their competence. Never was a performance so full of life and joy for me. Mel's question about my hands was the ecstatic antidote blending with the inspiration and pleasure of playing with Karen on the flute, then with Rosalie on the violin.

In the afterglow each night when the final chords have been struck, I settle in for the words. Alan stands to acknowledge the musicians, beaming at me, hugging me, and announcing that it is my birthday. He delivers his second night essay and I am so proud of him. He makes this amazing event happen.

Following the roads, images, and moods offered by Mel and Greg I feel full. Greg is delivering tales of his life and advice on how to live well. When Mel reads I am thinking of the rich and painful and complex relationship I have shared with him over about twenty years.

He is one of the only people I have ever dared and needed to fight with. He may have been, at times, my negative animus: brilliant, powerful, self-assured (Jewish) male to whom I have in times past given away my power. We have experienced varied terrain together. Climbing out of Coyote Buttes after dark, following a thunderous downpour, gingerly traversing slick rock up and down, three of us sharing one small flashlight; our sandaled toes assaulted by unseen cactus thorns. I covered Mel's head with my gortex hat to stop his teeth from chattering.

Years later, Alan, Mel and I are seated at our round table. Mel is angry at me and never wants to see me again. It feels as if I am fighting for my life; I am definitely fighting to preserve the friendship between Mel and Alan. I am the keeper of so many of Mel's inventions which I use in my life and my psychotherapy practice: "living-our-learning", the Taoist braid, seeing your true face, the tuning effect. I honor and respect this man and I battle to keep awareness of my "center" and my breath. We are both on fire for about four hours as we pour extravagant dessert wine down our throats just to quench the heat. My thighs are heavy and burning as we talk fiercely into the night. When it is all over and we limp off to our respective beds exhausted, I feel battered and deflated, yet oddly triumphant and empowered. As the weeks and months pass, we develop a real bond that is at once fragile and made of steel. It has taken years to break through our projections and our pain with each other but we have emerged with mutual respect, gratitude, admiration, and love, each crediting the other for our personal growth.

In contrast, Greg is my easy play pal. During the weekend we have ridden bicycles on the meandering roads, challenging ourselves to the bigger hills. Greg's heart seems so easy to access: we confide in each other, laugh, and climb. Later as Alan and Greg and I are lazing around, still warm from the spell of the week-end, he says "I love watching you two be married". Some of Greg's many gifts are savoring and sharing.

Bringing people and events and beauty to our area has been an ongoing intention and passion that Alan and I share. My lifetime struggle to belong, to be part of something bigger than me is fulfilled for this week-end. My friends and clients, some of whom I bullied and badgered to come are interspersed through the audience. Their amusement, engagement, and joy radiate. They forgive my relentlessness and they know we are all witnessing and participating in something good. Here, we all belong with ease. The poetry conveys a gamut of emotions. It feels acceptable and even desirable to be human. People are crying and laughing and visiting newly familiar places. Spring has finally arrived. Greenness prevails.

... so haben wir klüglich die grünende Zeit nicht versäumt, und wann is gegolten, doch glücklich geträumt im Grünen, im Grünen.

... if one day life will no longer grow green for us, we wisely will not have missed the green time, we will have dreamed happily in the greenness, in the greenness.

I am one-half of the professional poets invited to this festival, and I am standing before a polite library crowd naked. The audience smiles. They are not focusing on any particular parts, but are just pleased with my nakedness. Though the nakedness is not literal, the spiritual transparency of a skillful performer–musician, comedian, actor, poet—is nudity personified. Our job is to use our bodies—voice, movement, expression—to bring to life some body of work that connects to every person in the room. I am simultaneously terrified and liberated. I want to cover myself, but instead I look at the audience and smile.

Every practiced performer has a pre-performance ritual to move them from a state of nervousness to controlled ecstasy. For me, the nervousness before speaking in front of an audience is simply stark terror. The terror, however, is not a bad thing. It's essential. It's a form of energy, like Uranium-235. The key is to harness that energy into a slow even fission. Heat enough to run the plant, but not so much as to combust on stage.

And so you find performers who use various practices, activities, or substances to control the terror. For tonight, I spent the previous half hour prowling the library shelves, practicing yoga, running down aisles, glancing at a World Wrestling magazine and meditating in the children's section of the library, my knees up to my chest on the pre-school-sized chairs.

Just before the performance I searched for Mel, my fellow poet at this reading. Mel leads workshops and retreats, lectures at universities and medical school teaching healers how to heal minds and souls at places like Harvard and Esalen. He has presented many thousands of times and if there is anyone who is relaxed in front of a crowd, it is him. If I can touch base with him, I'm sure some of his confidence will rub off on me. But when I find him, he is leaning against a book cart looking nervous and overwrought. I touch his shoulder and he snaps, "Is this thing ever going to start?" I am taken aback—so much for words of comfort. But then I chuckle. No matter how many times you've done this, if you love it, you get nervous.

"Soon, man, soon," I say. And then, as Alan starts his introduction, I tell him my idea about how I'd like to do this. He listens and says, "I'm right behind you, brother."

Poetry is a lot like standup comedy. Both go before an audience, do their thing, and the audience either gets it or doesn't. On a good night a comedian touches the audience with some humor and insight, catches some laughs, and calls it night. A poet's good night is to touch the audience with some beauty and depth, and catch some sighs. A sigh to a poet is as laughter to a comic. The comic and poet both try to share their captured truths hoping to move some part of our audience.

For the audience, a good poetry reading is interesting images, ideas, some laughs, and maybe being touched by something given. A great poetry reading cuts through the dross and distraction of existence to the most heartfelt and important things in one's life. It can begin a self-conversation that reveals the hidden core of one's deepest longings, laments, emptiness, and desires. Conversations like this can change lives.

Tonight, with Mel, I want to go for the great reading. However, instead of keeping the conversation internal, I want to open it up. I want to see what kind of alchemical magic can happen when 70 people are opened up to those deepest feelings and articulate them into the room. I want to set the place on fire.

Alan completes our introduction to polite applause, then Mel and I take our places before the audience. Our pre-performance jitters are gone, and we are crackling. I start to speak and a cell phone rings. A woman leaps up, carrying the singing phone like a clicking Geiger counter down the aisle. I pause for a moment as she walks away, then continue speaking.

I explain to audience what poetry can be. How, if you are open to it, it can open your hearts to reveal things you may not have know. Things you need to know. I tell them that we are going to throw a bunch of ideas and images and feelings into the room, and that we want them to just take it in and see what happens. Mel tells them that after a while, we'll open the floor and see what's going on with you. He finishes by asking if they are willing to engage in this conversation. They agree. And so we begin.

I start with a poem called, "Ode to My Wife Who Mows Lawns." Mel reads "Heaven's Band." I toss in a poem about an aging jock sucking oxygen from a soccer boot. He throws in the southwestern desert night of wave foam constellations. I speak of the Cargo one must find and deliver in our lives. He speaks of a child's first discovery of creativity.

And so it goes. A swirl of ideas, images, passions and pursuits tossed into the room like logs on a bonfire. Mel is the wind and I am the flames. The audience moves, inwardly and outwardly, as if in a fever.

The room has become a crucible and the poetry is the fire. In this container, the leaden portions of our lives—our reserve, our rigidness, our held-too-long beliefs about the world and ourselves, our heaviness of heart—begins to soften and move. Folded arms fall to their sides. Mouths soften and drop. Their expressions have become the wide-eyed innocence of 3 year olds.

We stop, Mel and I, and take a break. A moment of silence.

"What's happening out there?" Mel asks gently.

An older woman speaks, she is shaking. "Your poem about American funerals reminds me that I when my mother died, I didn't cry. And I didn't cry when my father died, or even my husband." She pauses. "I think I would've been better if I had. But I just can't." Later Evie tells us that she saw her tearing up.

A younger woman stands. "That was my cell phone that went off earlier. It was a phone call telling me that my mother-in-law passed away. It wasn't unexpected, but I wasn't sure that I wanted to return here. I did because if I didn't, my friend would worry about me. When I did return I could feel what was happening. That this is just where I was supposed to be and that this is a passing ritual for her."

A man said, "I work with youth incarcerated as adults. I wonder if I could use your poem with them. I think it would speak to them."

And so it went. Instead of a reading, the library had become a sacred ritual space where people could feel the things they most needed to feel and share. As humans we need, at a very deep level, to share our lives in community. Not to receive advice, or affirmation, or even caring or love, but a simply to have others to bear witness to our lives. To bear witness to the pain and grit and joy and struggle that it is to be fully human. I share another poem.

Heart Attack

They say he died of a sudden heart attack at 64,
but maybe
he died of a broken heart from 64 years
of not feeling what he felt.
All those feelings packed down like brown sugar
in a coffee can.
Maybe
his heart broke because he would not
dance the dance his heart felt,
sing the song his heart heard,
love the way his heart loved.

Maybe his soul, trapped in that boney prison,
finally broke free
and put the heart out of its misery.
Maybe
people don't die of heart attacks,
maybe they die of broken hearts.

We allow a few more stories into the conversation, then continue with more poetry. We throw in humor, pathos, Eros, sadness—the elemental stuff of living. We pause for more conversation. The audience is alive with feelings and passions, their own as well as with everyone else's in the room. It is a stunning and beautiful thing when Mel ends it with his equally stunning and beautiful "Prayer for the Elements."

We receive our applause and as the meeting breaks up, we carry stackable library chairs to the storage closet, move library tables and chairs to their proper places. There is a sense of healing, fullness, completion, even ecstasy as the last people linger and mill about in the library, not yet ready to let go of what we have shared.

In April 2006 I partook in an effort with three others much like that of the musicians in Block's story.

This effort, The Power of Poetry, was organized by Alan Cohen and was for two imprisoned populations: men in the Southeastern Correctional Institution and the citizenry of the greater Logan Ohio area. The theme was Walking the Road of Beauty, an ancient Navaho theme.

Hopefully, we left these populations somewhat more enriched and joyful for our having participated with them to reawaken the song of vitality in their lives. It was an aesthetic mission of outreach and recovery. We were there to rescue and reinstate what vitality we could from the numbing anonymity of the imprisonment of a people locked in a prison for crimes committed, as well to rescue the vitality of people locked in the self-imposed prison of numbed conventional lives.

In prison we found men as sensitive as any other anywhere else. These men, mostly black, sat in their chairs, feet crossed, hunched forward, hands laced together, muscles twitching around their mouths, eyebrows furrowed: powerful horses bridled against their will. An atmosphere of resigned despair.

If you open your emotional awareness in such a setting, you find there is a morbid fascination thinking about living in prison. The world is monochromatic, monotonous, for the most part one gender, (except for some staff), and no exit.

Your sense of privacy recedes to a smaller and smaller space within you. Day after day you learn a new version of pain, the necessary numbness of solitude and isolation that comes from losing contact with the constant newness and change happening in the outside world. This can be your first reckoning with the fact that your life has been stopped from choiceful movement.

I was stunned by the following, repeated voluntarily and separately by several men: "I couldn't stop myself. I had to be stopped. That's how I got here". I heard this around the circle of inmates sitting in the room. They came to learn how to use poetry to give their bottled up feelings voice; their feelings of frustrated resignation.

The drug dealer from Chicago read a piece, like rap, that he dramatized powerfully, feeling more and more relieved as he read it, others nodding in agreement with his way of telling.

Another read a piece with more rhyme to it, sing-song and monotonous, somewhat preachy, with a biblical style. Again, more nodding. We encouraged them, offering different styles and teaching them how to recognize each style's way of carrying a different feeling. Then we had them try their hand with the new forms. Now some stifled tears came, some laughter, some sad reflection.

Alan Cohen has been going to this facility for ten years, introducing Joseph Campbell's mythology, poetry, self-awareness approaches so that these imprisoned men could have ways to humanely rehabilitate themselves, ways to reclaim their lost voices and souls, ways to express their need to be known to themselves and others in ways the regimented world around them did not provide.

We brought them the instrument of poetry, a way to build a voice to let their frustration stand outside themselves, to let the sense of beauty re-inform their lives with balance and meaning.

A version of what the poet Theodore Roethke meant when he wrote: *"Art is the means we have of undoing the damage of haste. It's what everything else isn't."* We conducted two sessions at the prison, morning and afternoon. The first session was us leading a large group; we performed for them. The second was more intimate, smaller and closer with much more give and take, all of us talking together.

Then we began two evenings of readings for those self-imprisoned in the everyday world. It was held in the town library. Alan's wife, Evie, a clinical psychologist in Lancaster by day and remarkable artist and musician the rest of the time (when not redrawing the state's highway system by long distance bicycle riding) performed marvelous Schubert piano pieces. Culture comes to small town Ohio. The audience was not merely polite, they were bursting with enthusiasm. Why here, why now, why free, why us?

My colleague, the ingeniously playful poet Greg Kimura, performed his marvelous Cargo poem, another about his wife mowing the grass. We played off each other like jugglers, our give and take like high level sport. Loving, energetic and fast repartee'. People were softly surprised: is this poetry? It doesn't rhyme. I like how it makes me feel. The second night's response was larger, more exciting, animated, engaging.

What really happened and what's really important about this?

It goes back to Roethke, art repairing the damage of haste, and to the essay Alan asked each of us to write and post on the conference's website in anticipation of arriving there in April.

He asked us to write about what happened in our childhoods that changed our attitudes to appreciating poetry in spite, if that was the case, of the way we may have been 'forced' to learn it in school.

The real answer to the importance of Alan Cohen's Power of Poetry Conference is the grass roots nature of giving ordinary people tools and experiences to let them feel empowered once again to re-inherit the initiative to express their vitality first, not learn how to succumb to the surrogates of vitality our society enshrines, cynicism and pain.

This is a gift example of what anyone can do and, as Stewart Brand wrote so well on the cover of the first Whole Earth Catalog: *"We are as Gods and should get good at it"*. We are not Gods, but AS gods. And like the Whole Earth Catalog described itself as an, "Access to tools". The Power of Poetry Conference provided access to tools.

And finally, as David Brower reminded us editing the important Sierra Club format series of books, introducing his, *Everest, the West Ridge, "We are not proud enough of being alive"*

These are noble sentiments. True.

But until we have clear models of how to bring experiences like the Power of Poetry Conference into prisons and communities at the grass roots level, all that remains of noble sentiments are words without legs to walk into the worlds of our lives.

Do not our lives pivot on the point defined by Steven's crucial lines?

*"The greatest poverty is not to live
In a physical world,*
**to feel that one's desire
Is too difficult to tell from despair."**